Cowboys, Plowboys, and Country Folk

By
Roger Ringer
Illustrated by
Martha Brohammer

Cowboys, Plowboys, and Country Folk

Country & Cowboy Poetry
by Roger L. Ringer

Additional contributions by Charlotte Ringer
Copyright © 1998 by Roger Ringer
Wildfire Ranch Productions

All rights reserved.
No part of this book may be reproduced
in any form without the permission of Roger L. Ringer.

First edition, Sept., 1998
Printed in U.S.A.
Printing Inc., Wichita, KS

ISBN 0-9667507-0-5

Distributed by Wildfire Ranch Productions
1660 S. 343rd W., Cheney, KS 67025

Illustrations by
Martha Brohammer © 1998, Clearwater, KS
All rights reserved.

Cover by Martha Brohammer

Typesetting and Editing by
Mary Brohammer, Lawrence, KS

About the Author

The first five days of life is the nearest Roger Ringer has come to being a "City Boy." Since that time he has lived in rural Sedgwick County, Kansas. Soon after graduating from Goddard High School he became a firefighter for Sedgwick County until a disability forced his retirement. On and off he can be found working on farms and ranches for family and friends. His roots are deep in the soil. He calls himself, to quote Baxter Black, a "poor dumb ole day worker." He is also an accredited auctioneer.

With a deep faith, love of fellowman, music, and country, it came natural for him to put his feelings on paper. Thus, he became a "Cowboy Poet." He has read many of his award winning poems at Old Time Poetry Gatherings in Wichita, Kansas, the National Cowboy Symposium in Lubbock, Texas, the Pony Express Museum in St. Joseph, Missouri, as well as many local gatherings. Roger is also a freelance writer; *American Cowboy* magazine published one of his articles in June 1998.

About the Artist

Martha Brohammer was raised on a farm in rural Douglas County, Kansas. She graduated from Baldwin High School and went on to receive her Bachelor's Degree in Art Education from the University of Kansas. She has taught Art and Spanish in Missouri and Kansas and currently, as Mrs. John Roach, teaches both subjects at Cheney USD #268.

Table of Contents

1. Cowboys, Plowboys, and Country Folk 1
2. The Gatherin' 3
3. Day's End 4
4. Jesse's Trail 5
5. Tornado 7
6. Annie Laurie 9
7. Sheep's Clothing 11
8. Ole' Merle 12
9. *Kansas One-Liners* 13
10. Garden Plain Nicknames 14
11. Modern Cow Camp 16
12. A Cheap Barn 19
13. Lonely Grave 22
14. Just Passin' Thru 24
15. Old Bill 25
16. Grandma Holley's Stove 27
17. Friendship 29
18. Five Acre Landlord 32
19. A Prairie Gathering 34
20. History 35
21. Kid Cowboy 37
22. When a Cowboy Hits Forty 39
23. The Day the Hero Died 41
24. Poppin' Brush 43
25. Ann Marie's County Fair Project 45
26. Foreboding 47
27. Arena Wreck 49
28. *Cowboy Definitions* 51
29. Florida Feeders 53

30.	Stomped	55
31.	Turtle Digging, Part One	57
32.	Turtle Digging, Part Two	58
33.	*Cowboy Truisms*	60
34.	Big Discovery	61
35.	Golf Huntin'	63
36.	Deliverance	65
37.	Horse Sense	67
38.	Mist on the Greenleaf	71
39.	*More Cowboy Definitions*	73
40.	Spring Calving	75
41.	The Legend	77
42.	Prairie Love Song	79
43.	Passin' Along	81
44.	Redjaw Coyote Hunt	83
45.	*More Kansas One-Liners*	86
46.	A Birthday Visit	87
47.	Rounding Up the Strays	89
48.	Big Red	93
49.	*Still More Kansas One-Liners*	95
50.	Silent Night	96
51.	*More Cowboy Truisms*	98
52.	Snaky	99
53.	Nightmare	102
54.	Openers of the West	106
55.	An Old Cowboy's Final Comment	109
56.	Dad's Shop	111
57.	God Don't Like Mobil Homes	114
58.	Dance at the Grange	117
59.	*Still More Cowboy Truisms*	118
60.	Big Daddy's Last Harvest	119

61. *Still More Cowboy Definitions* 121
62. Full Bloom 123

"Mom's Things"
The Poetry of Charlotte Ringer

63. Memories of Mom 125
64. Big Daddy 127
65. Quilt of Love 128
66. Bucky's Christmas Visit 129
67. True Friends 131

Illustrations

1. Grandpa Ringer x
2. Cowboy of Color xii
3. Tornado 6
4. True Friend 28
5. Darrell 31
6. Kid Cowboy 36
7. Ann Marie's County Fair Project 44
8. Ranch Hand 52
9. Golf Huntin' 62
10. Les 70
11. Pinochle 74
12. Ranch Hand's Gal 78
13. Passin' Along 80
14. Prairie Dog Dave 92
15. Range Rider 101
16. K.O. Huff 108
17. Dance at the Grange 116
18. Plowboy 122
19. 'Round the Campfire 130

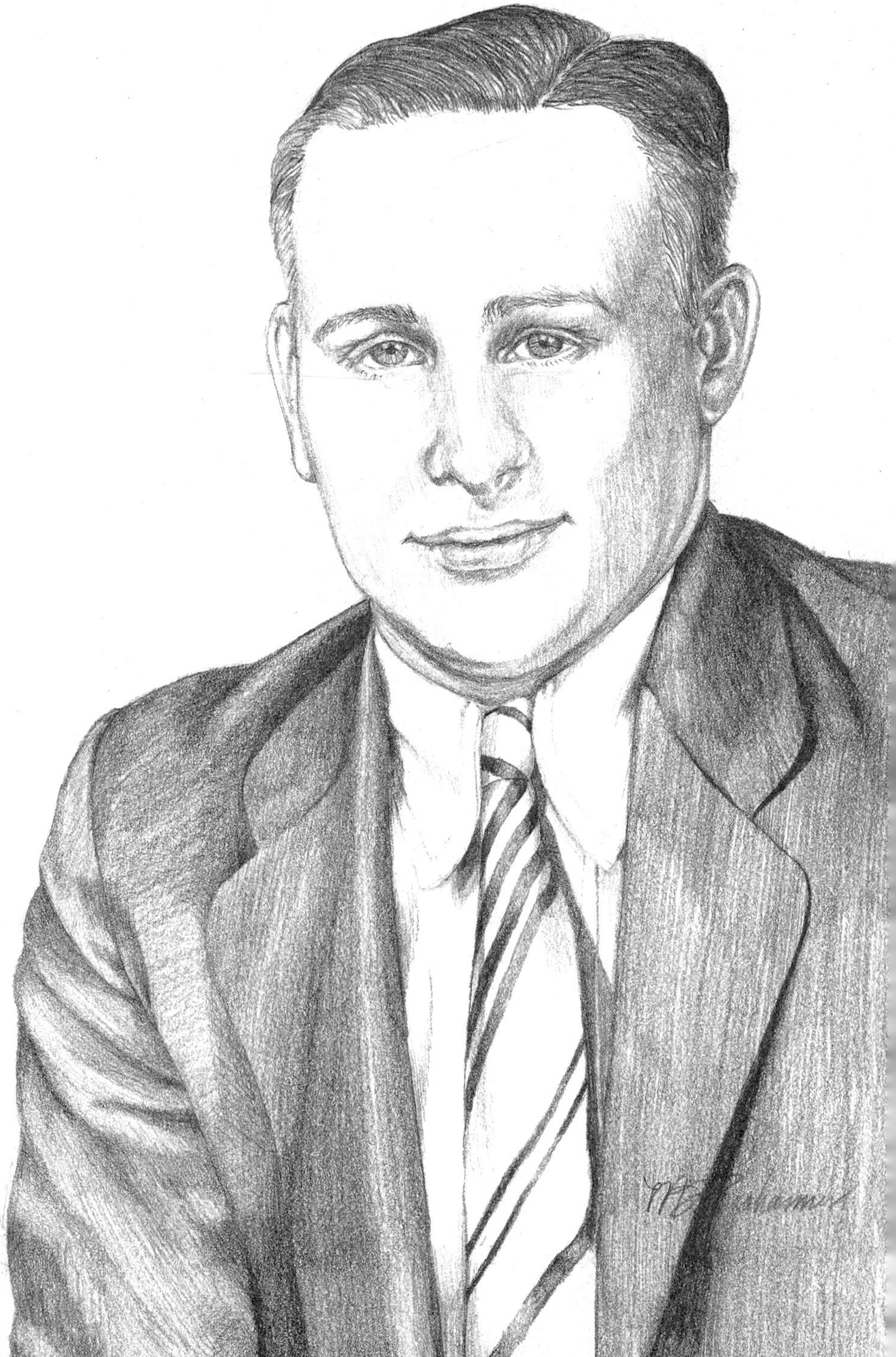

Dedication

This book is dedicated to the memory of some very special people who I miss terribly and wish were around to share this with me.

Grandma & Grandpa Becker (Mae & Carl)
Grandpa (Lloyd) Ringer
My best friend, Darrell Nieses
Joe Schauf
Big Daddy (Frank Kyle)

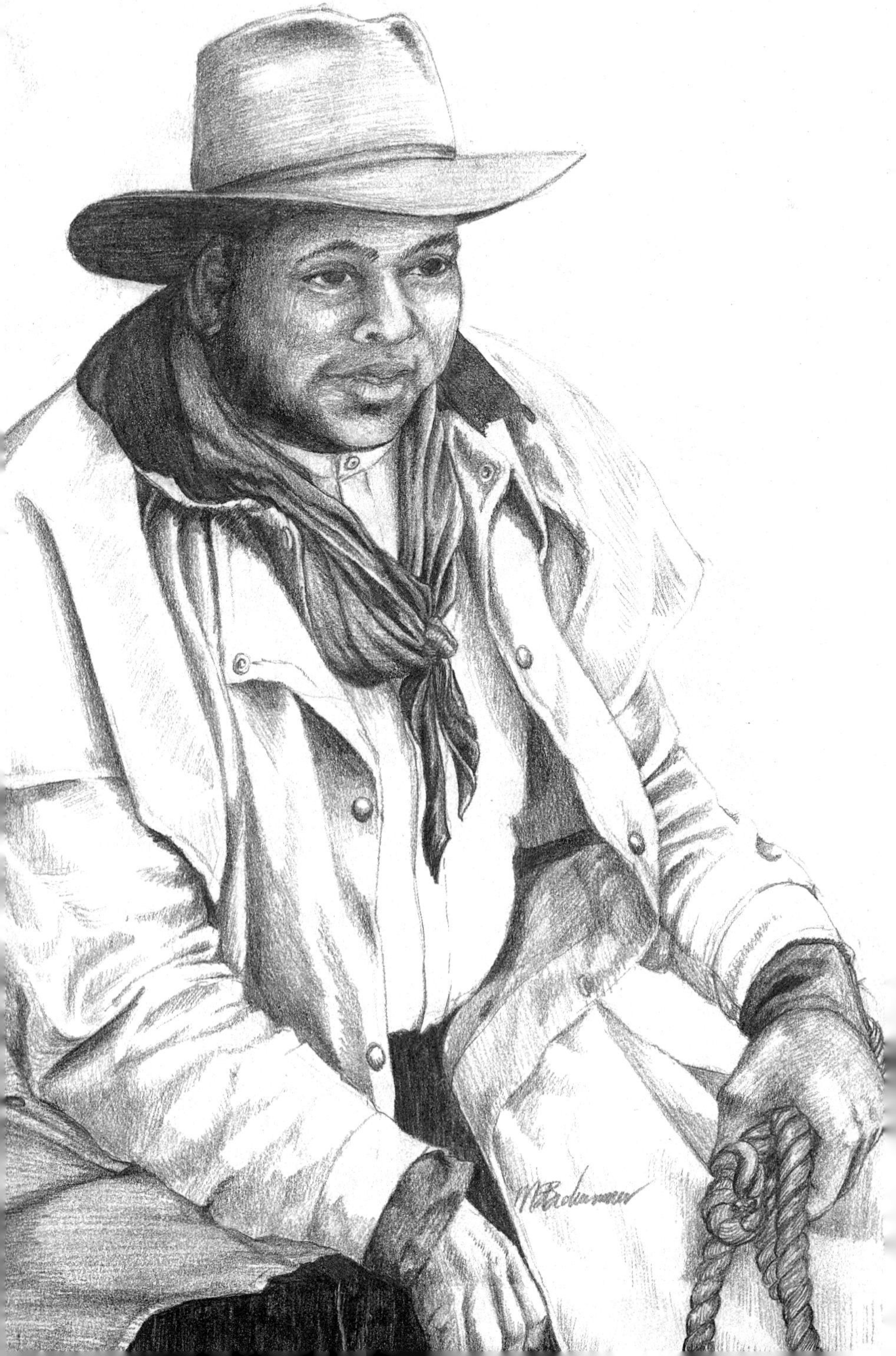

Cowboys, Plowboys, and Country Folk

Travel, if you will, to the ends of the earth,
All kinds of people you will meet.
Each one has a story to tell
And most will if you wait long enough.

Most live in a world that is not your own . . .
Their values to you they will quickly impart.
Many will judge you as you appear . . .
And try to convert you if you don't quickly depart.

When I feel myself losing my grip
I feel the need to take a trip
To a people who welcomes you as you are.
I look for Cowboys, Plowboys, and Country Folk.

Cowboys, Plowboys, and Country Folk,
People who live near the earth,
Wherever you roam they are waiting at home,
Those Cowboys, Plowboys, and Country Folk.

Some people chase the almighty dollar,
Others seek elusive fame.
You know, some of them think we're insane,
Us Cowboys, Plowboys, and Country Folk.

If it's wisdom you seek . . .
And answers to the world condition,
Everything is available to the meek
At the cafe morning communion or afternoon sessions.

At the feed store the old men
Will point out your mistakes
And laugh at the times
When by a trader you're taken.

Cowboys, Plowboys, and Country Folk,
Where people live near the earth,
Wherever you roam they are always at home,
Those Cowboys, Plowboys, and Country Folk.

Religion you can find down at the church
But God's cathedral is all around
And you discover that simple is best
And by love and honesty you pass the test.

Yes, Cowboys, Plowboys, and Country Folk,
Where people are the salt of the earth,
Wherever you roam they are always at home,
Those Cowboys, Plowboys, and Country Folk.

The Gatherin'

There's not many places left today
where history still survives . . .
not relegated to memories . . .
that with a person dies.
Or, into a book that they seldom read . . .
for the lessons that history teaches . . .
people seldom heed.

But those of us who still believe . . .
and try to keep history alive
are often seen at gatherings of this kind . . .
with an urgent need to tell what has been . . .
and pass on traditions before they disappear again.

We'll tell ya stories that make you laugh . . .
and tales that make you cry . . .
spin yarns of heroic deeds . . .
and talk of how cowards die.

Somethings we describe will be accurate as can be . . .
then, imagine some that's silly as you will see . . .
cause, sometimes you need to laugh . . .
or not be ashamed to cry.

If you take the time to come to see us . . .
I know you'll be back again and again . . .
to be a part of the past . . . coming alive . . .
at the cowboy country poet gatherin'.

Day's End

Darkness has fallen over the valley
the cattle graze peacefully down there.
The moon is rising over the hill,
as the coyote sings his song of cheer.

The old dog answers back to his ancient adversary,
as a small fog raises over the creek.
A guitar softly playing in the bunk house
a tune of heroic deeds.

Sitting here on the porch after a long day's work,
satisfied with the steak from supper,
remembering the time gone by.
The bitter and sweet I view tonight.

Though I've not much in the way of worldly goods,
look at the riches I've got.
I work every day in the Lord's cathedral
and sleep under a sky of angel dust.

Jesse's Trail

This trail was not new when it was staked . . .
for generations many knew the way
it made travel easier to take
over the south central plains.

Though once it was finally laid out
it came to bear Jesse's name.
And, the many legends it spawned
would forever gain it fame.

Many a trail had to be blazed
to build this great nation.
But, among all the trails
the Chisholm was the greatest sensation!

It wasn't real narrow . . .
it was a wide swath thru the plains.
The men who worked upon it didn't know they'd be legends,
legends we treasure today.

Now, you can compare this trial with all the rest
what makes it shine was what it gave . . .
It turned a poor working man into a legend . . .
It gave the drover a name . . . and the world a hero.

It's now been plowed under and paved over . . .
but the legend we celebrate . . .
"The Chisholm Trail" lives on today,
a tribute to the cowboys who made it great.

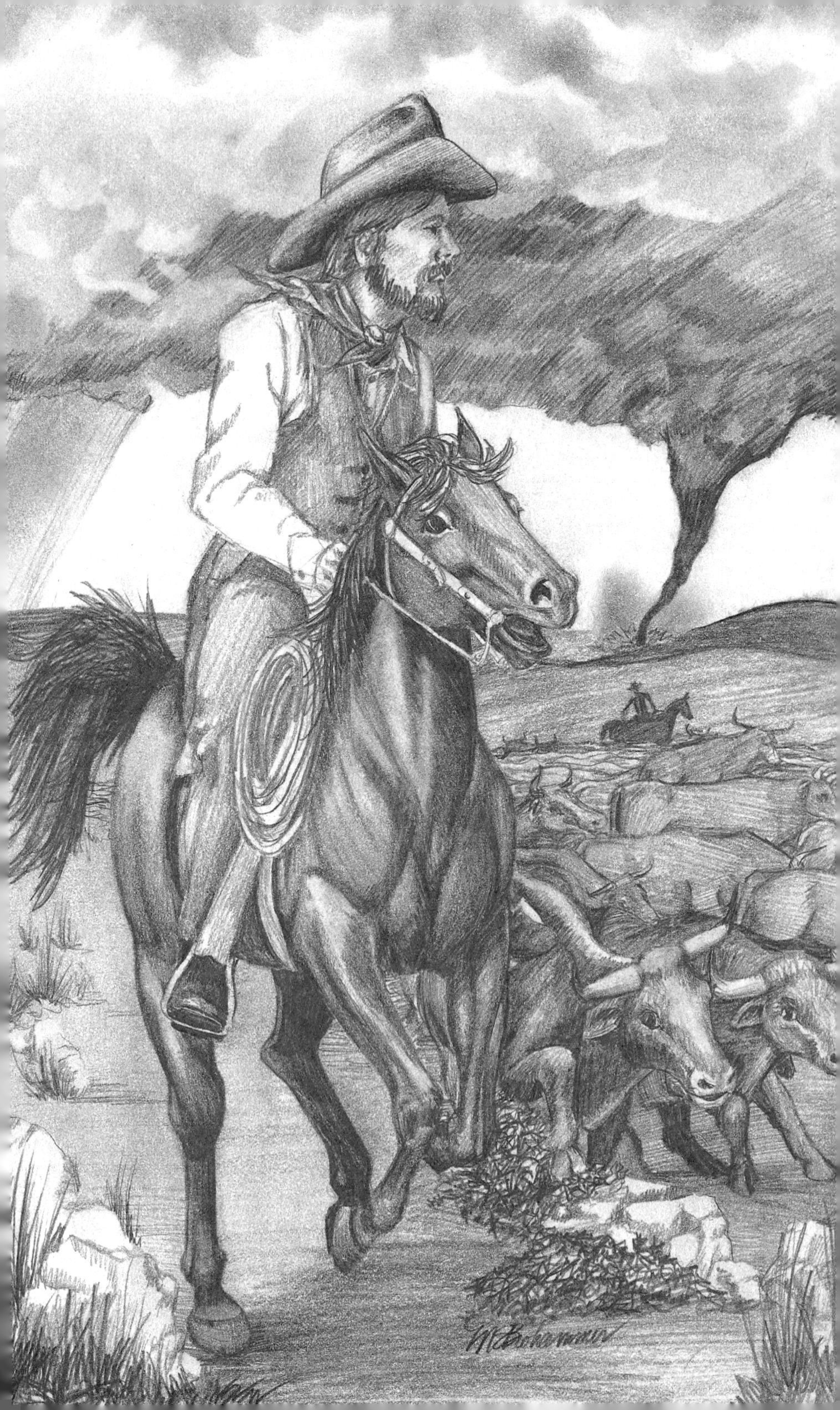

Tornado

It was hot! I mean downright oppressive at that. There weren't even enough breeze to shoo a gnat.

Me and Jim were holding a herd trying to add a little gain before we shipped to market in Old KC on the train.

Along about midafternoon ole Jim says in a haunted voice, "Storm's a brewin' as sure as hell. We need to start pushin' this herd. Find a better place to weather it out instead of being a lightnin' rod on this plain."

Now the wind had blowed hard for three days and nights in a row. We were all on edge, being experienced with Kansas weather all the signs were plain as sin.

If we didn't move soon there would be hell to pay.
A boomer was brewing on this fertile plain. It was sure by nightfall things would violently change.

When a cool breeze touched my cheek I turns and looks southwest. The blackest meanest looking clouds I have seen in all my days!

"Jim," I says, "we're a mite late. As I calculate we better run 'em northwest and cut the path. Get 'em over the bluffs by the slate."

Then it got still, as still as can be, then hot again, then a roar like a train. That big black cloud started to narrow down. It was the biggest tornado I have ever seen.

I've seen twisters in my time, this thing wasn't in the same class. This damn thin put a hurricane to shame. It looked to be two miles across.

We started a stampede to try and cut across the path of this storm from hell. To get over the bluffs was our only chance. You can't outrun them very well.

It was hell bent for leather, the most terrifying ride of our lives, sweating blood and praying Old Buck wouldn't spill. Racing the devil for our very hides.

We topped the bluff behind the herd, thankful when we hit the valley. The storm was roaring in my ears, I jumped into a buffalo wallow.

The longest minutes of my life, to tell the truth I was scared clean thru. I lost ten years of my life that day and what I saw I'll never forget.

We made it with most of the herd. I mounted and started to count. Looking for old Jim to see how he made out.

Jim didn't answer when I started to shout. We were only ten short. I was set to go to town and celebrate us coming out. But Jim was nowhere to be found.

They found him early the next night some ten miles from the bluffs. He was a terrible sight, it really shook the boys up.

We buried him on the spot. Still shaken by the mess. The way he died that way still haunts us to this day.

When it storms anymore I think of Jim and remember that fateful day. When my life started all over again. Jim left and I was chosen to stay.

Annie Laurie

In an old saloon that last night
feelin' a bit excited for what ahead of me lay . . .
settin' out to trail a bunch of steers headin' north . . .
when a man set down with one last song to play
. . . called Annie Laurie.

That sad old song left me lonely
and, as I went on my way . . .
from the hurricane deck of a horse
as the endless boring miles I sway
. . . I remember Annie Laurie.

Goin' to the bed roll early . . .
after evening chuck
I drift to sleep a listenin'
to that night herder, Old Buck
. . . singin' Annie Laurie.

When I'm rolled out for my watch
'round the herd 'til morning light
plodding along slowly . . .
I sing to the critters real light
. . . about Annie Laurie.

Day after day . . . for endless miles . . .
night after night . . . for endless rounds,
it stays with me all the while
in my mind . . . the haunting sound
. . . of Annie Laurie.

To my friends I say,
as around the campfire we're found,
if any ill should befall me, . . .
over my bones, as you gather 'round . . .
. . . please sing Annie Laurie.

Oh, that sad haunting sound . . .
thru life where e're I'm found . . .
rememberin' the trails I've been down
that tune in my head comes around
. . . Annie Laurie.

Sheep's Clothing

He looked and talked the part
A seasoned buckaroo with lots of heart
He throwed his riata with competent grace
He cinched up good and tight

I thought his riggin' looked a little new
Despite the coat of dust
His moves seemed a little practiced
His words and attitude a little smart

Now among cowboys it's quite a varied lot
One may sign with an X
And another may know Greek
It takes all kinds to make up this breed

But no matter how you handle your words
You have to know cow to succeed
Compleat your tasks nice and neet
And use a little sense

The boys got all over me for sendin' him off alone
To work a hand short would be hard on us all
And every hand would be put to the test
But I knew my boys were among the best

I says "You know you can't judge a book by its cover
On this ride we need no pretenders
I knew he was a greenhorn when he tolt
That he carried six shells in his old Colt."

Ole' Merle

Just the other day down to the cafe
I was sittin' in on the Liar's Club
many things of the past were discussed
milkin', breaking sod, bucking broncs.

When I mentioned to Merle a story he told
about his younger days and riding broncs
a look came into his eye, I could tell that a memory
had just come alive.

He smiled and said yes I broke 'em when I was young
and the first year they had a rodeo at Pretty Prairie
I went up and entered the show.
Bareback, he said, your own riggin'
not like the ones today.

First time up I won he said
and the second night was the same
he said after that he had to quit
to ride another time he'd have to join the turtles.

I had other things on my mind you see
and going on the road wasn't fittin' in
and the way life turned out
I was right.

Now Merle is retired and moved in by town
his son and grandson run the place
but I think he was still a bit proud
to be the first amateur bucking champion at Pretty Prairie.

Kansas One-Liners

It gets dry in Kansas . . . how dry can it get?

The label on the Coors can are all rocks cause the springs all dried up . . .

The Schlitz Malt Liquor cans are empty cause the bull drank all the suds . . .

When there's a fire they turn all the dogs loose from the pound.

Had a 12-incher a while back . . . drops were 12 inches apart.

The creek filled up and drowned all the fish . . .

We don't put mudgrips on our trucks . . . they're dust paddles.

Garden Plain Nicknames

It's been said over in old Garden Plain
that no one is ever satisfied with your given name.
Now I've been around too many an old town
and when I sets and ponders it,
I've never been to a place where
everyone had a nickname.

Seriously, I don't know the reason
or have any explanation as such.
Might be the water
or maybe the heat.
Thar's many ways of lookin' to it.
And if you come by the situation is perplexin',
you might even come away with one of your own.

Now thar's Chief who runs the station since '53,
and Shooter who gets one drink of whiskey
and goes plum crazy.
Years ago there was General Boots and Doc.
And here recent the Lord called Joe, Slim, Mule,
and Big Daddy.
We sure miss them all alot.

There's Flash, Snips, and Tater,
Duck, Monkey, and Whiskers.
Fast Eddie and Fuzzy.
Make er Smoke Bobby.
The brothers Tuffy and Mucho.
And if you need a new mower the Guvennah
will sell you one when he gets the notion.

An Toby, Dutch, and Digger.
Pinky, Lefty, an Cotton.
Pancho, Uncle Vic, Jack and Jerk,
and even a dog named Kitty.
Brother Elton, Brother Paul.
Midget and the Lion Tamer,
and I'm sure I've made some misses.

It's a cast of characters I'll garauntee.
You'd think I might have got this all out of a book.
But I swear it's all true
Provin' that thru and thru
Fact is stranger than fiction.

So if you're ever near old Garden Plain
Stop by the station or down to Dick's.
Set in on a game of Buck.
Or Pinochle,
and have a few rounds on us.
And just maybe, if we like you,
you might leave with a different name.

Now you ask if maybe I have one?
Well, I'm proud to say,
Sometimes a handle won't stick and Sparky didn't last.
But then fate reared up its ugly head,
after riding out my rollin' pickup
and not windin' up dead,
now they just call me Old Tumbleweed.

Modern Cow Camp

Without a doubt in this here modern age
Ranch life was surely going to change
with all the newfangled trinkets and toys
I guess it stands to reason
that the cowboy could not stay the same.

The boss's son went to college and got an ag degree.
His daughter, who could break a cowboy's heart,
went into animal husbandry.
The boss man as sincere as can be
wanted to run the place more efficiently.

With gooseneck trailers, air conditioners,
Fourwheelers and cradles hydraulically driven . . .
FM radios, mobile phones,
Fax machines and computers . . .

It's all a bit overwhelmin' to the boys
that are still pushin' the cows.
But the thing I think affected them the most
was the day the satellite dish arrived from town.

With much trepidation and skepticism
the boys at the bunkhouse looked on
The boss man told 'em quite seriously—
"It won't take long to catch on"
this should be real interestin'.

In these days of labor movements
and rising social conscientiousness
it figures to keep you all entertained and informed
about all this worldliness.

Well it started out as a novelty,
its influence growed and growed
it started causin' some problems
the boss man could not have knowed.

Like Jake who got hooked it seems
on the Oprah Winfrey Show
started suspectin' his girlfriend's uncle's
second ex-wife of all kinds of unseemly acts
and really likes odd things to smoke.

Billy Joe who was watchin' a Greenpeace show
started talkin' about a hole in the air zone
animal rights and alternatin' lifestyles
then, joined PETA and tried to let all the calves go.

Buck got a bit randy
started sitting up all night
watchin' movies with stars named Candy
must be about candy kisses . . . each one was rated triple X.

Then, Jim started to cookin' things we never ate before
said it was cajun and cantonese and French . . .
it made ole cookie a bit PO'd
when we started callin' him "Chef Horny Toad."

Well, everything is shore different without a doubt.
I guess it was bound to happen . . .
last week we got into a fight at the bar
and had to "Kung Fu" our way out!
Called ourselves the powerful rangers.

Traditionalists downheartedly say
that things were all better in the "good old days,"
but then, like my Grandpa used to say,
"Good old days, hell" . . . I wouldn't go back a minute.
The best invention yet . . . is still the flush toilet!

A Cheap Barn

The rancher set down in the chair, looking a little nervous and upset. The banker looked worried and said, good to see you Jake, but what makes you fret.

Your calves did well, better than I expected, and you got them to the auction in plenty of time and hit the market high at 109.

Your grain looks good and the hay's all in, the co-op's been paid, the tractor is repaired and the government check was on time. You've even made your pickup payment, so why are you here?

Well, Jake drawled, it's a bit embarrassing, but I run into a scrape. It seems that a barn I been building has the county bent all out of shape.

A barn? I didn't know. You didn't come borrow. Jake says, yes I know. But I had this plan that would not cost me much. And I would end up with a cheap barn.

I got the lumber from the house I tore down over on the Johnson place. I saved the light fixtures and even the bulbs, the doors, and windows for light.

The siding I salvaged from Holley's barn that the wind blew down last spring. The only thing I figured to buy was nails and tin for the roof.

I was almost done when a car drove in with some guy I didn't know. On the side of the car was a county sticker that said Public Works.

He introduced himself as the county inspector and said I was in trouble. Trouble says I, I don't know how, been minding my own business here building my cheap barn.

Now there is the problem he says real grim. I see a new barn, now let me see your permits. This county's zoned, you can't build you a barn without the proper permits.

He said let's see I'll tally the damage and see how much you owe. The footings I see were poured with no inspection. No permit? A ticket for that violation.

That electric line isn't up to code and neither are the fixtures in thar, you needed an electrical permit. Another ticket for that violation.

I see in the corner thar that antique stove that was outlawed in '72. No permit for mechanical, another ticket fer that violation.

I see a hydrant you buried there I don't think you know the situation. No permit for plumbing, another ticket for that violation.

For not submitting blueprints for the fire marshal's inspection. No permit, another ticket fer that violation.

So you see, I had to come to the bank and borrow to pay off my fines. I had no idea that building a cheap barn could cost me $10,000.

My God, said the banker, I had no idea that the county could fine you that much. Jake said well, that includes my lawyer and my bail to spring me from the jail.

Jail!!! Yells the banker, just for no permits? I have never heard of such a thing. Jake smiled as he explained. Well, the fines on the permits amounted to just a couple grand.

The rest is for breaking his jaw when he told me to tear the durn thing down.

Lonely Grave

Heard a tale from long ago
'bout a long forgotten grave
in a windswept corner of Vinita Cemetery.
A grave where no one goes.
I sought the stone to see if it was true
and just as I was told
the stone . . . a simple message told "hanged."

No information on this miserable soul
was offer there 'abouts.
I wondered what the local committee
had used to decide his fate.
This area of the country
has always held tales of its many outlaws
and the vigilance committee that thinned them out!

Was he a desperado that deserved his gruesome fate?
What was the crimes that he did perpetrate . . .
was he a two-gun cowboy, or a drifter
that simply got in the way.

The answers may never be known
for dead men hold no council.
His time was his own and mine far apart
I look at the crimes today
and justice that simply looks away.
So, I turn to go on my way.

I turn and look back and speak to the grave
as if the outlaw could hear.
If you were innocent, I'd say "too bad"
and feel sorry this day.
But, if you were guilty, "good riddance to you"
for, if you lived today,
your reign would live on
with no one to cut your stay.

Just Passin' Thru

Gettin' born in this world
is like buckin' out for the first time
on a bronc no one has ever seen . . .
his moves are fresh and unexpected . . .
no one to give you advice . . .
not knowin' the moves he'll make when freed.

You ride loose and by instinct . . .
matching his every twist and turn . . .
sometimes you'll make the clock . . .
other times . . . ya get dumped in the dirt!
But the important part is doin' your best
every time out of the chute!

Life can throw twists and turns . . .
but like that buckin' bronc, he's just passin' thru . . .
one time you're up and win the buckle . . .
another time a mouthful of dirt!
Sometimes you'll even get hurt.

But, take what you get, and do your best . . .
even in failure . . . hold your head high . . .
so, at the end, you can say . . .
I tried my best every time . . . It's true
at the end, they can tell those gathered . . .
one last ride to go . . . 'cause he's just passin' thru.

Old Bill

The auctioneer said "sold" in a gravely voice
and the Little Greenleaf to a new owner was passed.
The end of an era and start of a new.
As all things in this world are bound to do.

It wasn't a big spread, so's you'd note . . .
nestled in by the Plum thicket and Chain . . .
but, for as many years as anyone could note or tell . . .
The head buckaroo boss and foreman was Old Bill.

Small and wiry, he walked a bit stoved up . . .
without a doubt he was the real mccoy!
Took him to be in his seventies . . .
but, me thinks that's about 20 years shy!

Without a doubt . . . a fact of life . . .
years of ridin' and ropin' take their toll . . .
this job of a cowboy ain't easy on a man . . .
when he's passed his youthful goals!

The man said to the new owner, in a serious tone . . .
you notice the condition of the spread today.
You need yourself a top hand . . .
a man who'll ride for the brand . . .
besides, Old Bill comes with this place!

So that's how I come to know Old Bill . . .
while dayridin' for the Gregory brand . . .
and I knew with one look . . .
here stood one of American history's living last stands.

So, when they talk about the glory days . . .
And the riders who made the ranches great . . .
I always picture Old Bill
like on a black and white glass plate.

Living history that slipped from the books . . .
so classrooms never would know him.
So, as the native from the past who had no books
or writing . . .
Old Bill can only be kept alive as legend . . .
in the stories that I'm tellin' . . .

G lazy G

Grandma Holley's Stove

When I was no more than a pup on the farm
I remember very well our neighbor folks
Just down the road west . . . 'bout a half mile
was a world of old machinery on which I loved to play.

Barns so packed with wondrous things,
pasture full of red cows . . . on the South Fork Ninnescah.
Ida and Lee weren't any relation you see,
but I called them Grandma and Grandpa anyway.

There were times when we would stay overnight
and in my mind my most remembered sight
was that Big White Oak Stove that burned
all through the night.

Now if you call it a wood burner
I'd dispute you and raise hob
cause it always burned from a pile out back . . .
nothing but dry corn cobs.

When the wind blows at night
and a chill runs down my spine
I remember back to those wonderful times . . .
when I curled up under a handmade quilt
and was lulled to sleep in the warmth of that
Old White Oak.

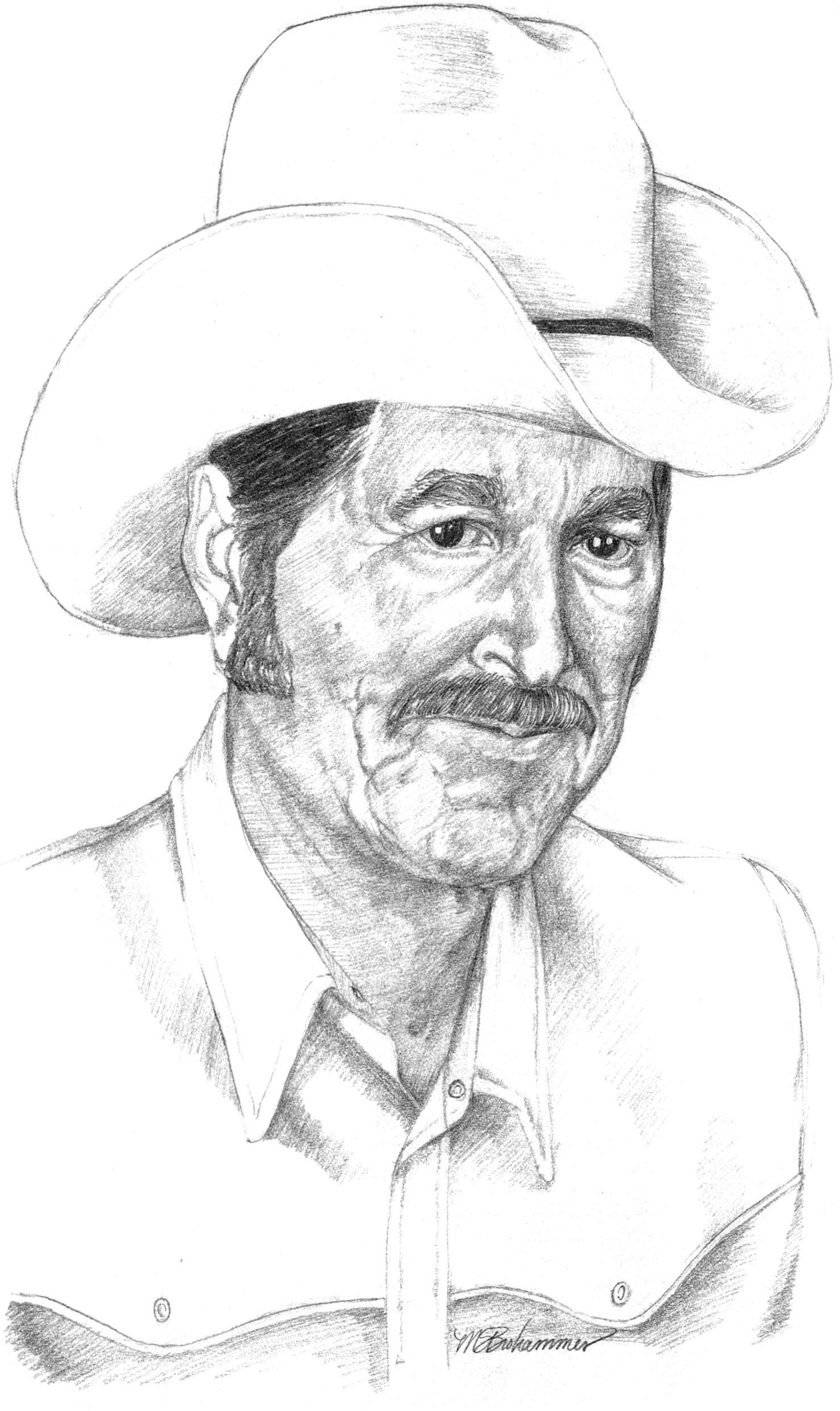

Friendship

Friendship . . . is a peculiar thing . . .
It's just not something you plan.
You can't just up and say . . .
I'm gonna befriend this woman or that man.

That's not to say you can't be a friend
to everyone you meet . . .
The Good Book tells us to be friends to all.
But . . . that's not exactly what I mean.

Sometime in your life you have a best friend.
Someone special . . . it's hard to say when, how or why . . .
You accept it . . . it grows as each day passes by.

It's even said that if you have one . . .
Or, even two in your whole life through . . .
You're really the lucky one . . .
'cause that combination's so rare . . . only God can spare . . .
such a special one for you.

It's just that a friend makes life easier . . .
They fit like a glove or an old boot . . .
You can talk or do whatever . . .
They really don't give a hoot!!

But, as with everything that's good . . .
You pay a terrible price . . .
One day it will slip up on you . . .
and treat you with such contempt . . .
You'll cry to heaven . . . Why Me?
But silence is all you get.

You took it for granted . . .
Thought it would always be there . . .
You turned around and it's gone . . .
Just vanished . . . leaving emptiness and despair.

You wish the emptiness would just slip away . . .
Guiltily you utter . . .
There's so much I needed to say . . .
But can't . . .

But you know that friendship is still with you . . .
every day of your life . . .
It lives on in your memory . . .
It sill carry you through good times and strife . . .

Now, when your journey is over . . .
And you look up to the pearly gates . . .
Guess who'll be waitin' and sayin' . . .
What took you so long . . .
Been waitin' here . . . watchin' for you all day.

DARRELL

Five Acre Landlord

I've spent my whole life living in the country and loving every minute of it. But lately there seems to be a trend that I only half understand. It bothers me more than a mite and today, if you can stand it, I'll get up on my soapbox here and start to expand on it.

It seems that city folks are plum fed up with the ways things are in the towns, so they discovered my country and are movin' out in droves. Seems they enjoy listening to cricket squeeks, and cows that moan, and coyotes howling at the moon.

I was running a coyote just the other day and happened to meet one of these neighbors here. Instead of howdy and offerin' a hand, he looked square down the twin barrels of a shotgun and lectured me on the virtues of coyotes and other such affairs.

Now I was not hearing much of his lecture. I says, now mister, you take your fingers offen that trigger. Then he starts tellin' me if he had his way, he'd take all the guns like the one I wore and melt 'em all down into a block.

I was hopin' that the sheriff would not be as usual in takin' his time to get here. The longer the fool talked, the madder I got and considered jerkin' my iron, causin' the problem of two major cases of lead poisoning—his and mine.

He went on and on about us country folks and the way he and his kind would make us change. He'd quit us from running coyotes and make us pick wildflowers. Pave the road out front. And animal rights and vegetarianism and such.

It was providence I swear when the sheriff got there and made him put down his gun. He bristled and claimed his rights were infringed as he was the landlord of this five-acre spread he called the Ponderosa.

Now that I was free to speak my mind and get my two cents werth in, I took a deep breath and started to expand on the subjects he brought up there. Now I cannot blame anyone for trying from the city to escape. Myself for sure I would not stay, I don't have what it takes.

But before you come into my country and set up residence, scaring up the countryside with your trailer house, kids, and packs of pets, if you love my way of life so much, why do you want me to change?

Now I like dirt roads even when rough, and your cute little coyotes are a joy to listen to unless it's your calves and lambs he partakes. We like our wild flowers growing wild. And I will continue to feast on steaks, that's what I raise cows for.

And if you think I'll let you melt down my Grandad's Colt, you're sure runnin' amuck. If the way we live you do not understand, why not set down with a cup of coffee and ask me before you condemn all of us.

I like to know my neighbor by his first name, who he is and let him be. Then in turn I expects him to do the same by me. If you need a hand, give a call, and I will do the same.

And next time we run by your kingdom, your five acres we can pass by, for there are 635 others in the section, and I'd rather you get in and ride.

A Prairie Gathering

The sky was blue and the sun did shine
on our gathering today.
Some were not aware, even of the time,
grief can rob us that way.

On a bit of prairie by a little church,
a gathering of friends and family,
to lay a daughter, sister, and young mother
to sleep till time goes away.

A bitter draught indeed was served to all this day.
The eldest daughter by the eldest son . . .
both gone too soon. And we left to wonder,
shoulder the burden and go on our way.

A young padre with a burning soul
striving hard at our request
to make some sense of it all
and give our own spirits a rest.

Struggling mightily with its weight
shedding with us a tear.
He too was a friend conquering his own doubts,
struggling with his own pains and fears.

But time and faith heals all and blessing freely flow.
By us gathering here on this prairie parcel
we celebrate life, not death,
and with love strengthen each other's soul.

History

From time to time it happens to me . . .
Someone will come up and say why?
Why should it be so important to me . . .
That the past be kept alive?

Now I know that it is a part of life, and only right . . .
To respect others' points of view.
So I hear their opinions . . .
Then try to get them to see the light.

Knowing and respecting what has gone on before
Gives you a sense of place.
To learn from what's gone on before
Can avoid the same old terrible mistakes.

Why spend your life time a wastin'
Making all those mistakes again?
Learn from the past and go on,
Life a full life, my friend.

The basic elements of society are
honor, respect, and consideration.
And how do you expect to enter the future
without knowing the situation?

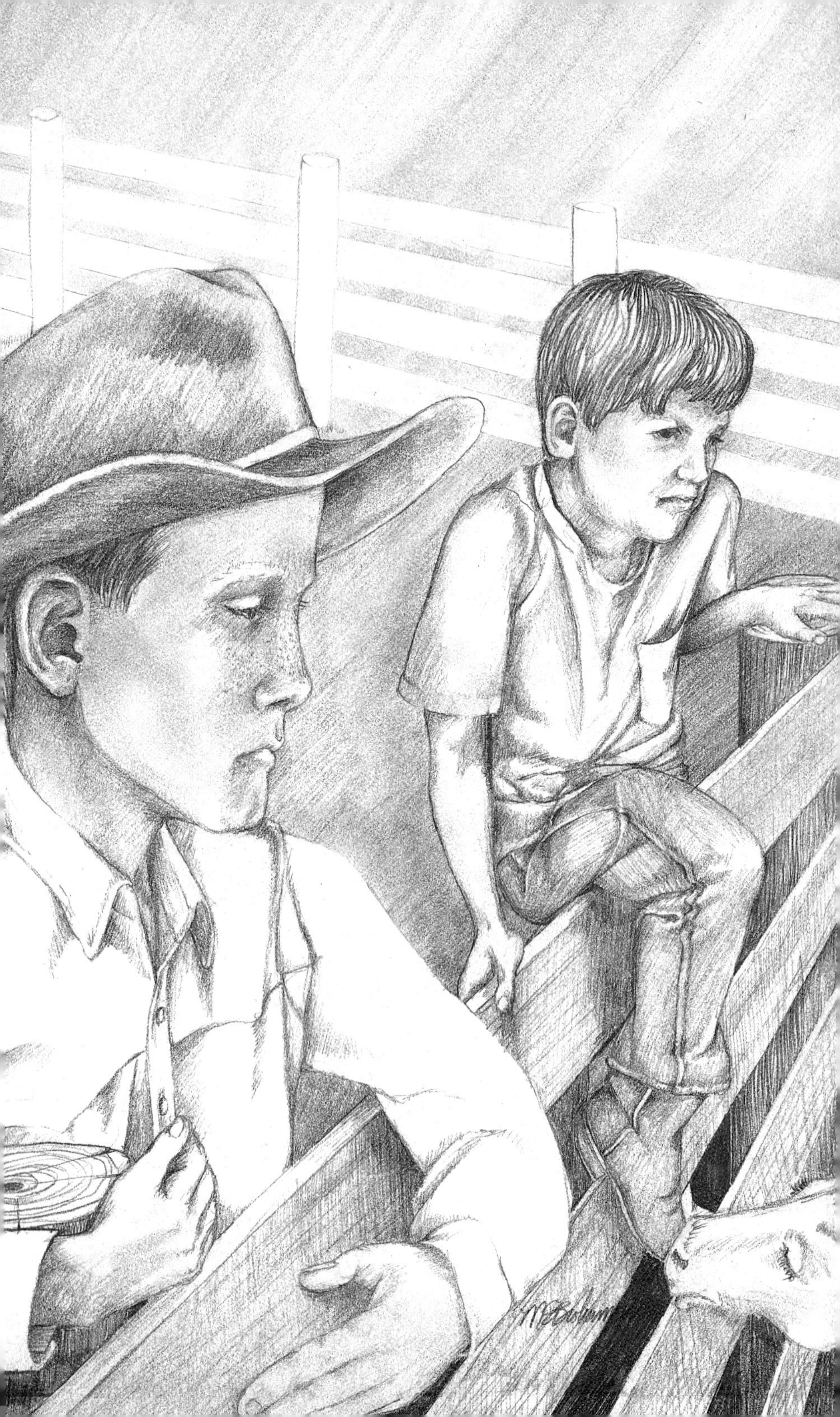

Kid Cowboy

He told his folks while just a lad, "I'll not be here long." They smiled and hoped it was a fad, "A cowboy's lot is where I belong."

As he grew, his friends turned to rock n roll, fast cars, an' dope. But he drove a truck and listened to Buck, choosin' to face life on his own.

His mother, she worried all his life long, about his chosen vocation. Hoping a doctor or lawyer he'd become, building a respectable life in some close location.

But he found his future at the end of a rope, dayriding for outfits out west. Learning his trade the hard way, trial and error, and success, for the life that suited him best.

Long boring hard hours, most can't understand. Poor pay, uncertain future. Broke down in the middle of nowhere. Busted up in a wreck, no pay till mended.

But he is living life on terms of his own, playing the hand he's been dealt. To many he's crazy, livin' on the edge. But living is what it's all about.

He could have sold out and plodded through life as most people do, not knowing the freedom of the road. Surrendering to safety and greed he knew would surely kill him and cripple his soul.

He seeks to find the void that God intended him to fill. And when he finds it, a steadier man you've never seen, settling into his lifelong dream.

He lives by a code. Be good to kids, horses, and dogs, and always give the Lord his due. The love of a good woman will temper his edge and treasure him all the way through.

So here's to that young buckaroo. Playing there on his stick horse may you ride off into the sunset. And to your dream, boy, always be true.

When a Cowboy Hits Forty

When a cowboy hits forty things seem a bit strange.
Seems that things that were, were
and now everything seems changed.

Seems like I have the same old dreams
and those dreams though they are the same
share themselves with other things.

When younger I lost track of the times I fell off the horse.
Now the thought of slipping on ice
fills me with remorse.

My pickup had four gears and a clutch
and drove with the windows down.
Now it slips into drive and the air conditioner blows on high.

I used to buck hay from dawn till dusk
then party all night . . . now round bales make good sense
and I enjoy sleeping at night.

The kid who hung around as a pup
is married now and breaks colts
and Segundo's a local horse ranch.

Outfits that used to work me through the busy times
don't call me anymore, . . .
But over coffee complain how hard help is to get.

I'd still like to have a little place of my own,
my own little spot of earth. But thoughts of interest
and mortgages steal some of my good intentions.

I was between angry and ill, the cowboy bad . . .
I listen to the people wonder of our youth,
they seem bewildered when they go bad.
What happened to the values of our youth?

My answer is simple to the bewildered
as preacher, doctor, and teacher wonder what went wrong.
Kill the hero and what do you expect
when he is replaced by ideological bullshit.

Poppin' Brush

Poppin' brush from dawn till dusk,
Pushin' ole longhorns in for the gather . . .
Dueling daily with horns that's sharp
And the temperament of a fighter.

Building a herd for the Driskoll boys . . .
The work requires lots of sand
Thirty a month and found . . .
They call me a "top hand."

I look forward to the summer
When we take the herd to railhead.
We'll pull into old Wichita town . . .
Then I'll cross over into Delano and sweet Lou Ann.

Curly red hair and eyes that's green,
Skin as soft as a summer dream.
Away from Delano, we'll flee
To a little cabin by a stream.

A ranch of my own on the Kansas plains,
A sea of grass over rolling hills,
A place for horses and cattle to graze
And, red headed kids to raise.

Day after day I rope and toil
With my horse and my rope coiled.
Poppin' cows from the brush
Working for my dream at the end of the trail.

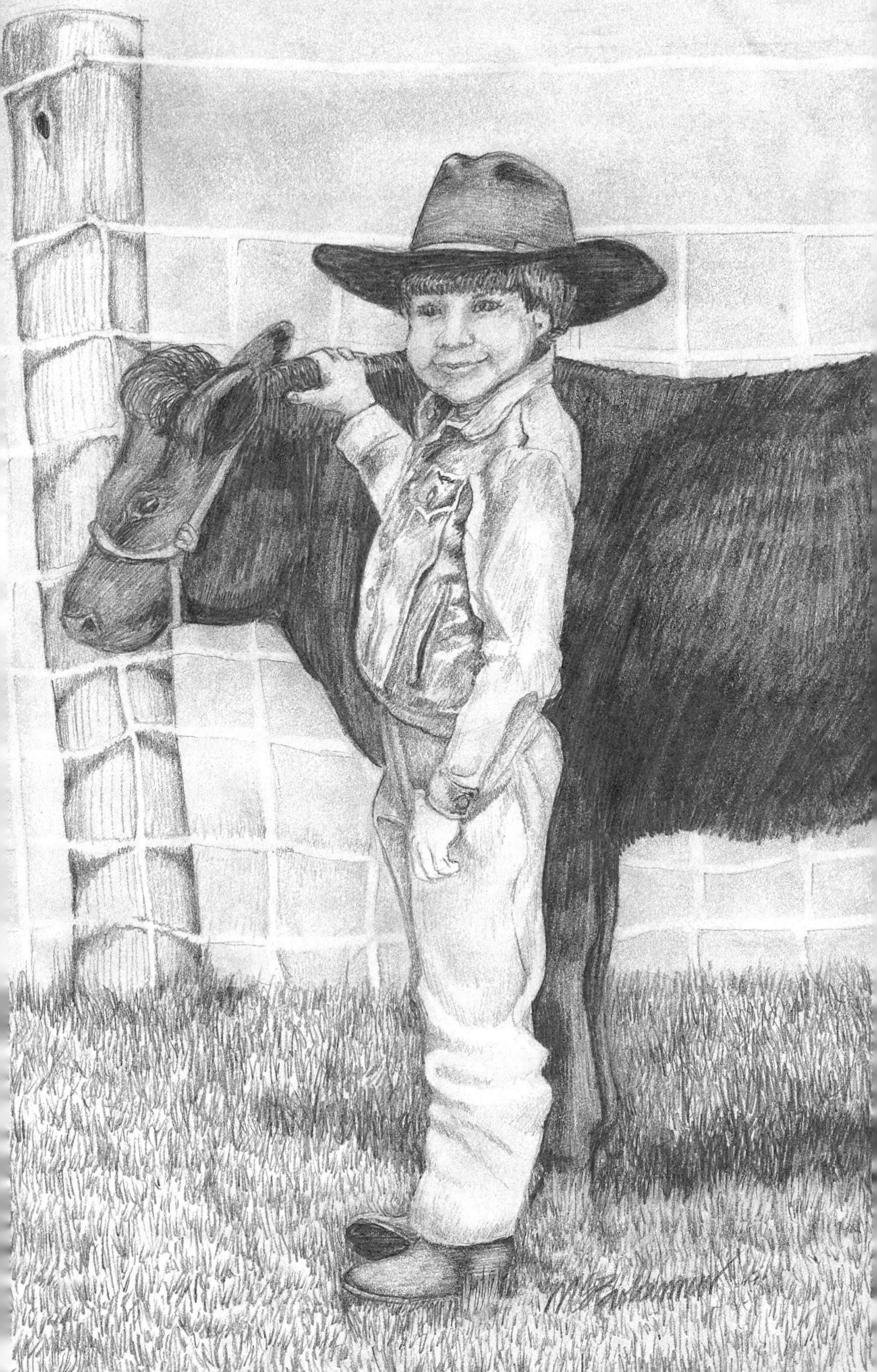

Ann Marie's County Fair Project

He didn't look like much just laying there
hide, hair, and bone that only a mother could love.
Wouldn't appear much like a champion
layin' in the grass kind of lazy.
But hell, he didn't ask to be born
gettin' up and moving around seemed plumb crazy.

Now Ann Marie rode out with her dad
lookin' the newborns up and down.
She was huntin' a calf for her 4-H project.
She looked at each calf with a critical eye
with the wisdom of youth she surprised old dad
when she chose this ungainly little spry.

He said OK, it's your choice to make,
but for the life of me I cannot see
how this excuse of a calf
even with all your tender loving care
can place in any competition
let along get you a blue ribbon at the County Fair.

But undaunted she worked with the calf.
She winced when they made him a steer,
groomed him and fed him till he'd follow her anywhere.
But with a halter he didn't lead worth a damn.
It was touch and go with one week to go
but givin' up was a word that she didn't know.

Well, it's all over but the shouting now.
That silly steer took a blue.
He performed like a champion should do.
Now at the auction he was bought
by Mr. Bauchman at 98.
This steer will help get her into K-State.

Standing by the trailer for a last goodbye
with her hair braided up
in her best blouse and jeans
her lip started trembling
and her eyes filled with tears
as she scratched his ear goodbye.

Proud of that gangly hard-headed calf
that brought out the best in her,
and now one last lesson he taught
that every buckaroo must learn to be true.
Of all things that are of this earth
only the memories last.

Someday I'm sure another little girl
will stand saying goodbye to another calf
and there Ann Marie will be to wipe away her tear,
just as her mother did for her.
An old blue ribbon she will bring out
and say, honey, I know it's hard
'cause I've been here myself.

Foreboding

The sun did not come up this morning . . .
It merely snuck into the town.
The birds were all silent.
The rooster made not a sound.
The chief of police got in his pickup
and made tracks out of town.

If you're from out of town,
and feel this evil foreboding . . .
take comfort in the fact that the locals don't fret.
You're always welcome, but do take warning . . .
hangin' around can play hell
with marriages, jobs and paychecks!

What is this evil malaise you ask . . .
is it somethin' predicted by an oracle?
Or, printed up in the Globe?
What is the source of its power . . .
is it good or evil . . . can it be avoided,
or is it listed in the chronicles?

I tell you this, it's not quite that bad . . .
I don't believe its roots are evil . . .
But, on this day, it has been known . . .
to have grandmothers, wives, daughters and sisters
all runnin' amuck.
'n if you're on the street, you might get run down.

Today the government stops . . .
the clerks are missin' from the stores . . .
secretaries are all gone . . .
commerce slows and all the streets are blocked.
The men folk open the bars early . . .
and won't venture out till dark.

For today starts the time-honored American tradition . . .
"Garage Sale Day" in Garden Plain . . .
Now Get Out of My Way!

Arena Wreck

One evening down to the arena we were honing our roping skills. I throwed a few loops and popped a few brews and caught an awful lot of air.

When Old Rose drives in and unloads a fancy piece of horseflesh we all gathered around to admire it 'cause we mostly rode plugs.

After a little bit of warm-up Ole Rose called my way, asked if I wanted to be the first to try this horse out and see what it could do.

Well, like a fish I took the bait though I should have known better 'cause I was far from being the best roper there. But I took him up anyway for, compared to my old mare, this horse was a millionaire.

I gits on up and builds a loop and backs him into the box. I nods my head to turn 'em loose and down the arena I shoot.

I swings once, then twice, and dropped the loop right on the horns. By this time I had visions of being a rodeo star. I daley up and git ready to drag and that's when the bottom falls out.

Instead of turning and setting that steer up for my heeler, he stopped dead in his tracks and backed up, but I was still moving forward across the horn.

I lay in the dirt, I know I'd been had and I spoke a few notes higher. A world class roping horse he surely was probably the best in his class.

But he was a calf roping horse and not a team roper. Old Rose and everyone else was laughing and rolling on the ground. Soon as I could I laughed with them.

Now there is one small lesson to be learned by my tale and it's not to be alert for sure things. It's that when you're around cowboys the tricks are all swell.

But just remember when you pull jokes the paybacks are goanaby hell!

Cowboy Definitions

Government employee: A person with a title and a condescending attitude determined to help you in spite of your ignorance (generally younger than you) . . .

Politician: A person duly licensed to lie, cheat, and steal.

Rat: A large furry rodent that will feed on your commodities . . . and foul what it cannot use. Refer to *Politician* . . .

B.S.: Multiple definitions that generally end up meaning the same thing . . .

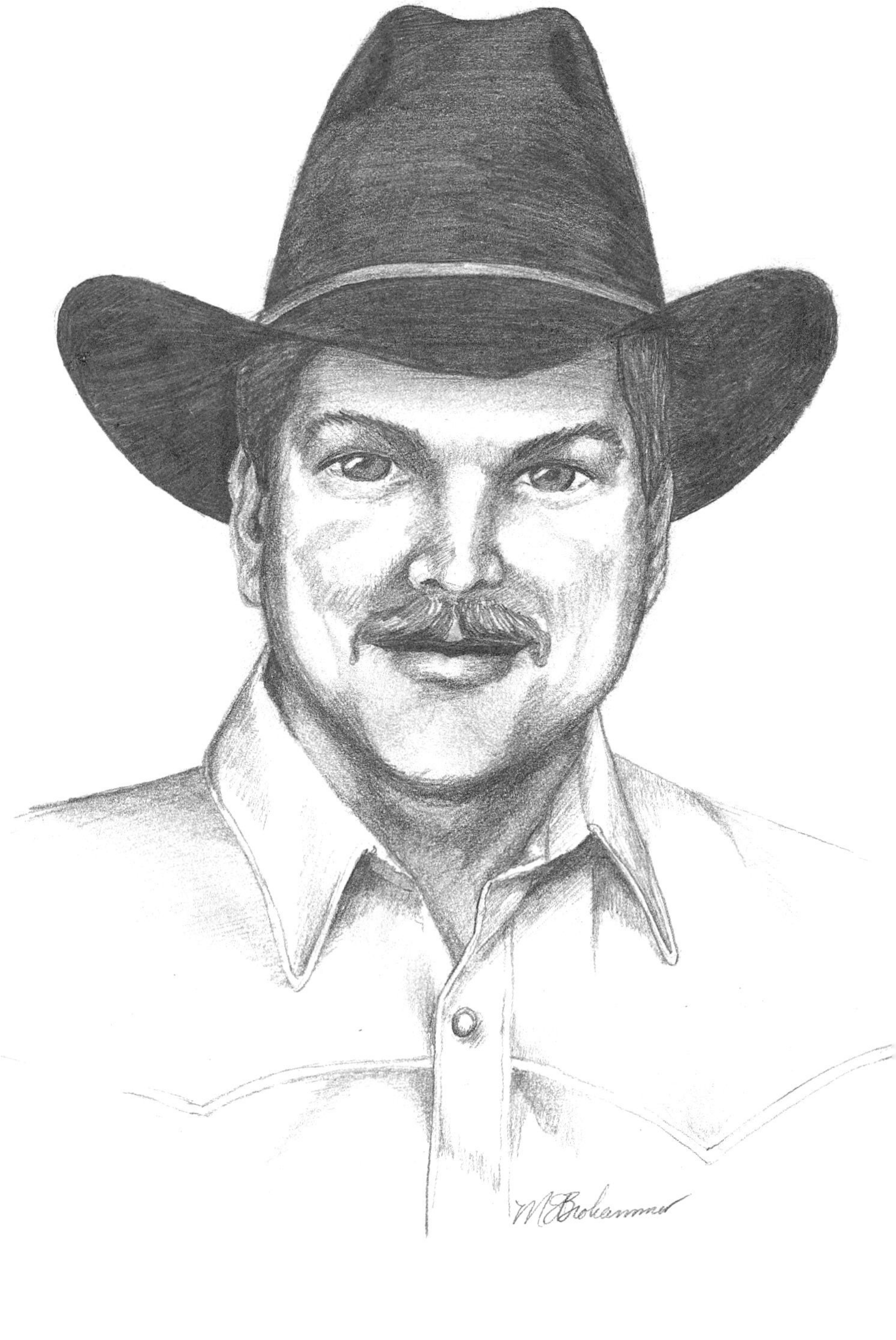

Florida Feeders

I was at Gregory's home place a few years ago
We took delivery of three pot loads
of Florida calves about 600 pounds
Eared calves they were all part Brahmer

A spookier bunch I have never seen
When you walked out in the yard
once seeing you there it'd be full speed
and hell bent to the other side of the pen

One night for reasons we know not
They stampeded north and laid down the fence
flattened out on the ground
just like it wasn't even there

That was a job bringin' them back
You could not move them slow
It was hell bent or nothing
If you faltered they left you to stare

They calmed down once just enough
to work them through the chute
Working them was bad enough
but I had to get in with them and push them through

Now I'm not know for silence
when running stubborn stock through a chute
But imagine how it was cussing each brute
when each one tried to take me with 'em through the chute

I whipped and prodded and cussed
was kicked, run over, and excreted on
Each one made a circle at least three times
before in the alley way they'd shoot

The last one of all of course was the leader of the pack
The craziest spookiest and meanest of the batch
He could just as high as I am tall
and kick sideways to take off my head

That worthless calf had every bad trait
and did his best my maker to meet
So I won't say I was sorry for his sudden demise
when he snapped his neck when the top pipe he did meet

I never enjoyed skinning out a carcass
as much as I did that day
and savor the patties I grilled
They were almost sweet I'd say

So if you have the chance to buy good Florida calves
remember they are raised by alligators
with dispositions of diamond backs
and antelope is in their blood line

You can set an example for your kids
when offered something too good to be true
just as they teach your kids at school
you can just say no to these too

Stomped

Damn you Saul, what have you done?
Last I recall I was giving you grain and then a freefall.
My ribs hurt and my leg is laying there. . . .
Saul, you devil brute, you stomped me sure.
I guess I got away rolling under here.

Under the feed bunk, I remember now . . .
If I don't get out of here real soon I could freeze . . .
What time, midday, I must of went out. . . .
You broke me up like doll rags, I've got to get out . . .
It's me or you, son, that's all there is.

I move and here you come,
come closer, you sun of a gun . . .
Draw out my old .45
I only got one chance . . .
If I miss I'm done.

Closer now closer now closer . . .
Starting to paw and charge.
Lowering his head . . .
Now cocking the gun.
The shot of my life and he is done.

Crawling dragging my leg,
Times like this I regret being alone.
At least my leg has gone numb.
Oh, she will be mad when I don't show up . . .
She will be mad as hell when I don't pick her up.

It's dark now, I made the yard, but must have passed out.
The moon is bright, freezin' hard tonight.
If I don't get in soon . . .
It wouldn' paid me to even start.
Boy, I think I will miss that gal.

I swear if I make it I'm goin' to propose . . .
I don't know what took me so long.
There is a bright light in my eyes . . .
I'm not so cold anymore.
I'll swear that was a kiss on my lips.

Now I got to decide am I alive or dead . . .
Another kiss, well I'll be, no I don't think . . .
If I'm dead things are mighty friendly,
If alive, someone must of heard what I said . . .
Well, either way I recon that there will be hell to pay.

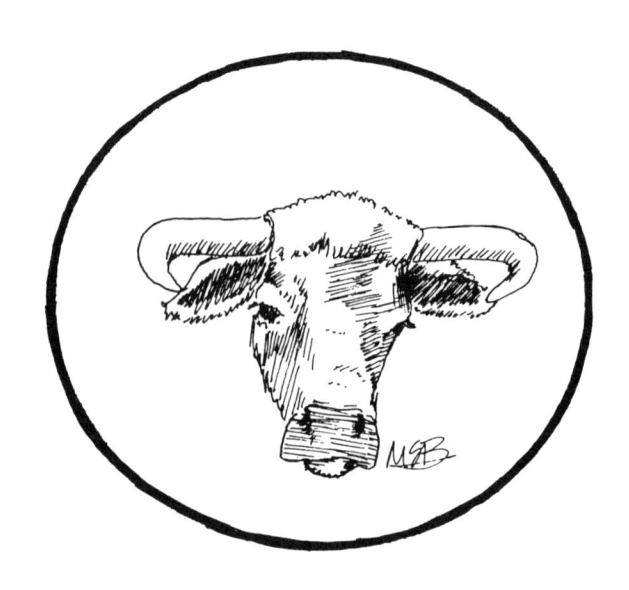

Turtle Digging, Part One

When the summer is gittin' along real good
and the Kansas sun will bake you to a crisp,
ambition wanes and boredom sets in real hard,
it's time for turtle diggin' to start.

Turtle digging, you ask?
Let me explain real fast.
The waters get low
and the big snappers dig down in the mud.

You get yourself a bundle fork
or an ordinary pitch fork will do.
Ice down the coolers and get a gunny sack
and go pick up the boys.

Load 'em up in pickups and head for the creeks and ponds,
pick yourself out a good shallow muddy stretch,
get in arms length apart and probe the mud with the fork.
If you hit something that don't feel like a rock, that's it.

Now you reach down and feel around,
feel the front back and sides.
It's important you get this part right
to save a finger or chunk of belly hide.

Now get a good stance and pull it on up,
hoist him high with no hesitation.
Now stuff him into the sack.
Nothin' to it, if you're quicker than lightnin'.

Turtle Digging, Part Two

Pull another round this heat is gettin' intense,
grass if failing, ground is blowin', milo's burning up.
I says to Big Daddy, a perfect August day,
ambition to do nothing but drink and play cards today.

About this time in comes Shooter carryin' a gunny sack.
Now we all knew what this meant, and we comes to our feet
as he dumps out a turtle on the floor,
a big snapper with an attitude, as most of them are.

He says with a grin, I found a mud flat and pulled him out.
Believe me if you're no good at dancing just throw a big
snapper out when you got your boots off trying to cool
yourself down from the heat.

The boys now have the fever and the doldrums disappear.
It's time to dig out the traps and forks and sacks,
get the cooler packed good and full
and a caravan heads out of town.

We pull up on a crick out on the ranch.
You cannot help but laugh at the sight
of these boys wearing nothing but cut off jeans and boots
and kids following with the sacks.

They work that creek with a vengeance, pokin' in the mud.
Shooter yell first and a concrete chunk is pulled out
and Gene is fighting off a water snake
when a yell comes from up the creek.

Larry grabs onto a turtle and asks which way is front,
made the mistake of believing Shooter
and pulls this turtle up to stare in the face.
He don't look for long as the turtle takes a chunk of his belly.

Now diggin' turtles is hard and dangerous work.
You may pick up a scar or two along the way,
but fried or smoked or soup
those turtles are mighty tasty anyway.

Cowboy Truisms

If you must ride a bull . . . draw a rank one. You don't get much respect gittin' stomped by a wimpy bull.

Treat every lady with respect . . . till she proves to be otherwise. Then avoid her like the plague.

Chewin' is one more item that a woman thinks she can change a man from doing.

Your world champion cowdog always performs best when no one is watching.

Big Discovery

The professor made his pronouncement
that the old west had ended . . .
Around the turn of the century
the cowboy at this time was dead.

The facts are argued among intellectuals . . .
the discussion is constantly renewed . . .
from books, papers, and seminars,
the arguments of the chosen few.

Should they accept history as told?
Or rewrite it all anew?
Shall they create a formula?
Like a mathematician would do?

They argue on and on forever . . .
searching for the answers anew.
Us common folk can't get a word in edgeways . . .
They just figured out the west of the movies

Just ain't true!

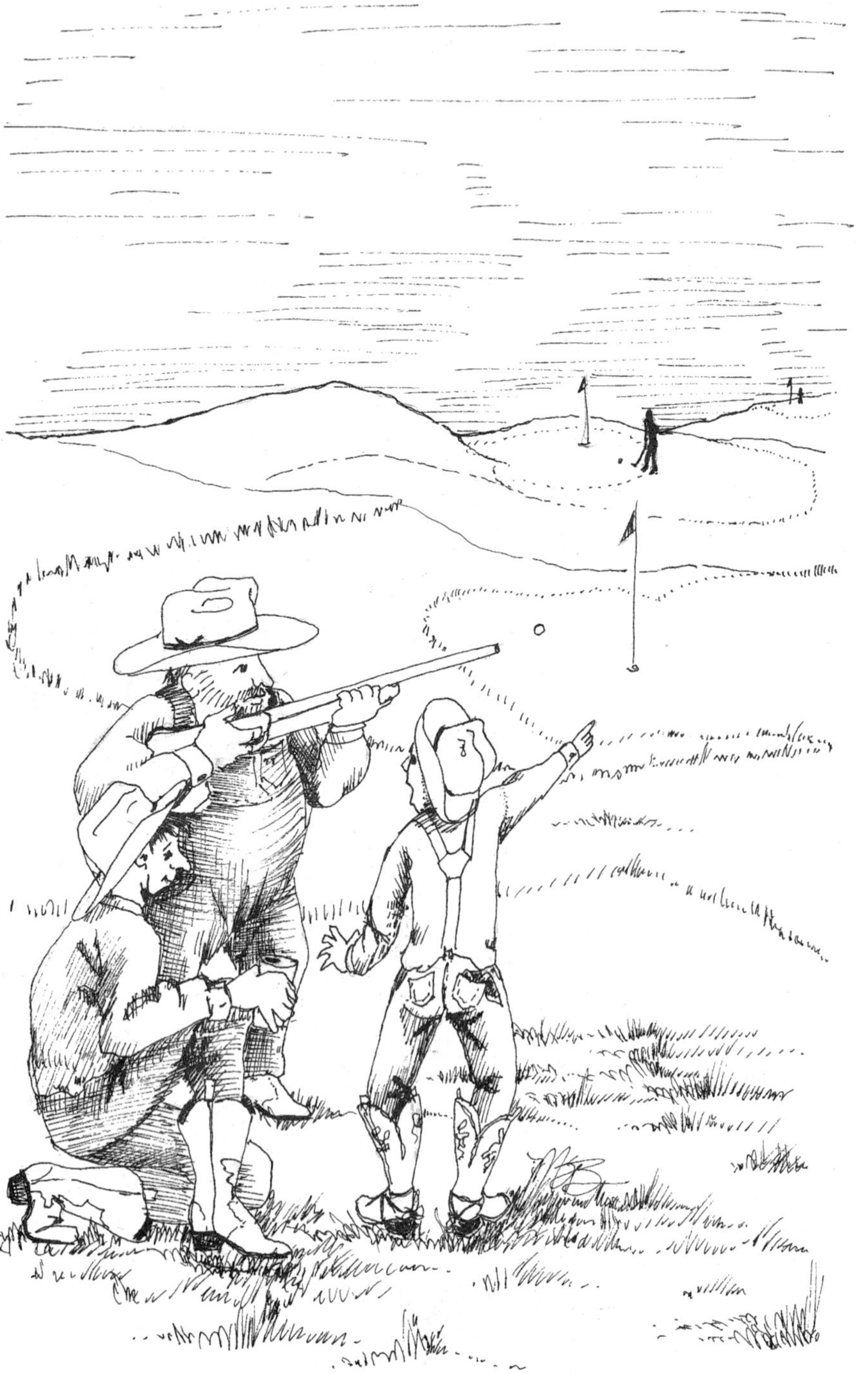

Golf Huntin'

Me and the boys did somethin' last summer
that we don't normally do.
We got done with all our chores
and headed into the city in the middle of the afternoon.

Now the only time we go into the city
is after dark on Saturday nights
up to the big dance palace
where in our Wranglers we wern't such a strange sight.

In the daylight things shore looked different
as we drove ourselves around town.
We found this great big green pasture
as lush as I've ever seen in the middle of a drought.

I stopped and yelled at this fella who was swingin' a big stick.
Asked him what this place could be rented for
cause we needed extra grass pretty bad, and besides
this place was plumb handy to the bar.

Well, he cussed us good and thorough,
said we made him mess up his shot.
I said, funny I don't see no gun. . . .
Then he said this place wern't for rent cause it was a golf club.

Now I didn't want to appear plumb ignorant,
not knowing what a golf was,
but I just couldn't pass up asking just exactly what a golf was.

We seen people all over the place
chasing these golfs with sticks,
some chasin' afoot, others riding' little white trucks.

Now I could see right away
that these golfs were cousins to prairie dogs
cause people would chase them all over
and beat on 'em with sticks
till they got away down their holes in the ground.

I said, boys, this is some sport
gettin' these golfs all in line,
but these dumb city folks got it all wrong.
Like prairie dogs,
we'll get 'em with rifles just fine.

Well, I started right in
and was doing quite well
when sirens started to howling right over the hill.
And these big city cops come down
and hauls us all to jail.

I asked politely what was wrong
but they just seemed to get madder . . .
madder by the minute.
The only thing I could guess was . . .
maybe I shot over the limit.

Well . . . we got out of jail . . .
lost my rifle to foot the bail.
Figured the neighborly thing that was wise
was to stop on the way back to the ranch
at the big golf barn to apologize.

But when we walked in some woman screamed
and people under their tables hid.
I says . . . we're not here to scare you all,
I just wanted one of the trophy golfs I shot
to mount on my wall.

Deliverance

Walking up to face the man a kid quickly going to the bad,
speed with a gun and false sense of courage the only edge I had.
About to face a legend to gain a bit of fleeting fame
in a wild and bloody land.

Believing the lies from a book that cost a dime
I broke ties at home and westward did roam,
unaware that the west that was wild
was past and a gunfighter a thing of tales of the past.

Dreaming of being a legend,
imagining my name with The Kid and Hickok,
I came to this town for a Marshall, famous for speed.
I passed the word that he had slowed with age
and when challenged would turn yellow and back down.

He came walking down the street slow with his Colt on his side.
A look on his face that shure wern't yellow,
stone cold eyes, grey and hard granite,
and when he stopped he showed no respect.
Not the way I had it pictured.

In a soft voice words that chilled my soul,
"A reputation, kid, is a damn poor thing to die for."
Here I was to live my dream and chance for fame and glory,
Now it dawned that I might lose this game.

"Kid, you should live a long life, there's adventures enough in livin'. You should live to share your tales with your grandchildren. Instead of a will-o-wisp filling a grave no one will remember, unmarked, another burden for the county to bury."

Mad for a moment and then I noticed his coat back . . .
Sun in my eyes and I never even noticed.
I jerked for my gun and as I laid my hand on it
his gun was leveled and cocked and on my chest.

"Son, it's up to you, a move and it's straight to hell
or stop and live to tell the tale."
I guess you know the rest,
I'm here to tell the tale.

There are many ways to seek glory . . .
and ways to build legends I learned.
I lived through no merit of my own,
standing at the gates of Hell when a ranger sent me home.

Horse Sense

Preamble: I have always suspected that these so-called dumb animals have a lot more on the ball than their human counterparts. We go round sayin' that this makes good horse sense. Or there ain't enough good old horse sense left. I have never heard anyone say that that makes man sense, or people sense. Most people I know gets their sense beaten into 'em. You know, gettin' a little arrogant and getting' their props knocked out. This here is an example of how I got a little edicatin of my own.

Now we were goin' to push cattle for the Broken Bar B
out in the pasture on the Garrison place,
a little piece of hell that is about as close to West Texas
as you can get in Kansas . . .
plum full of hedge and cockleburrs,
with a creek that winds back and forth.
We knew this were no piece of cake so we got extra help.

These cows came from Montana . . .
and you talk about a surly bunch . . .
they had to be part pheasant.
They hide behind a tree and flush behind you. . . .
This day was sure to be unpleasant.

That day I was mounted on Lady, from Hamilton's string,
a better old cowpony I have ever seen.
Into the tangle I rode some rank cows to chase,
I set into this place with a fury fore I knew this place.

The idea was to string 'em out and push them to the end,
bring them on up into the portable pens.

Now pushing this place meant fording that creek
every couple hundred yards or so . . . and it weren't
more than ankle deep any where that I knew.

The word was passed and the drive should start through
I urge Lady into this little pool . . .
and she stops and balks, not wanting to go in.
So I rants and raves and spurs her.

She just stands there, spraddle legged,
My temper was now something to contend.
I make her go on in . . .
Why, you would think it was quicksand.

She finally jumps, damn near leaving me behind.
We land in the center, stirrup deep.
Now I weren't expecting no crash,
boy that other side's looking steep.

I believe I said holy cow or words to that effect.
We ended up swimming to the other side.
And when she started up she rared and lost her feet
while I shout words of encouragement.

I give her rein and digs her flank,
then she lost her feet and rares up.
As she is coming over on me I do nothing rash,
just steps off to get away from this crash.

Now I stood looking like a drowned pup.
Lady stands on the shore giving me a dirty look.
I starts wading out a little worse for the wear
and shout to the boss to hold up, I am down.

I got into a mess, hold up the big press.
Down! he yells why we had not even begun.
So the whole crew comes over . . .
to laugh at the deed I have done.

A lesson well learned by me that day . . .
though the rider has got to be boss.
To avoid wrecks like that again
you have to be as smart as the horse.

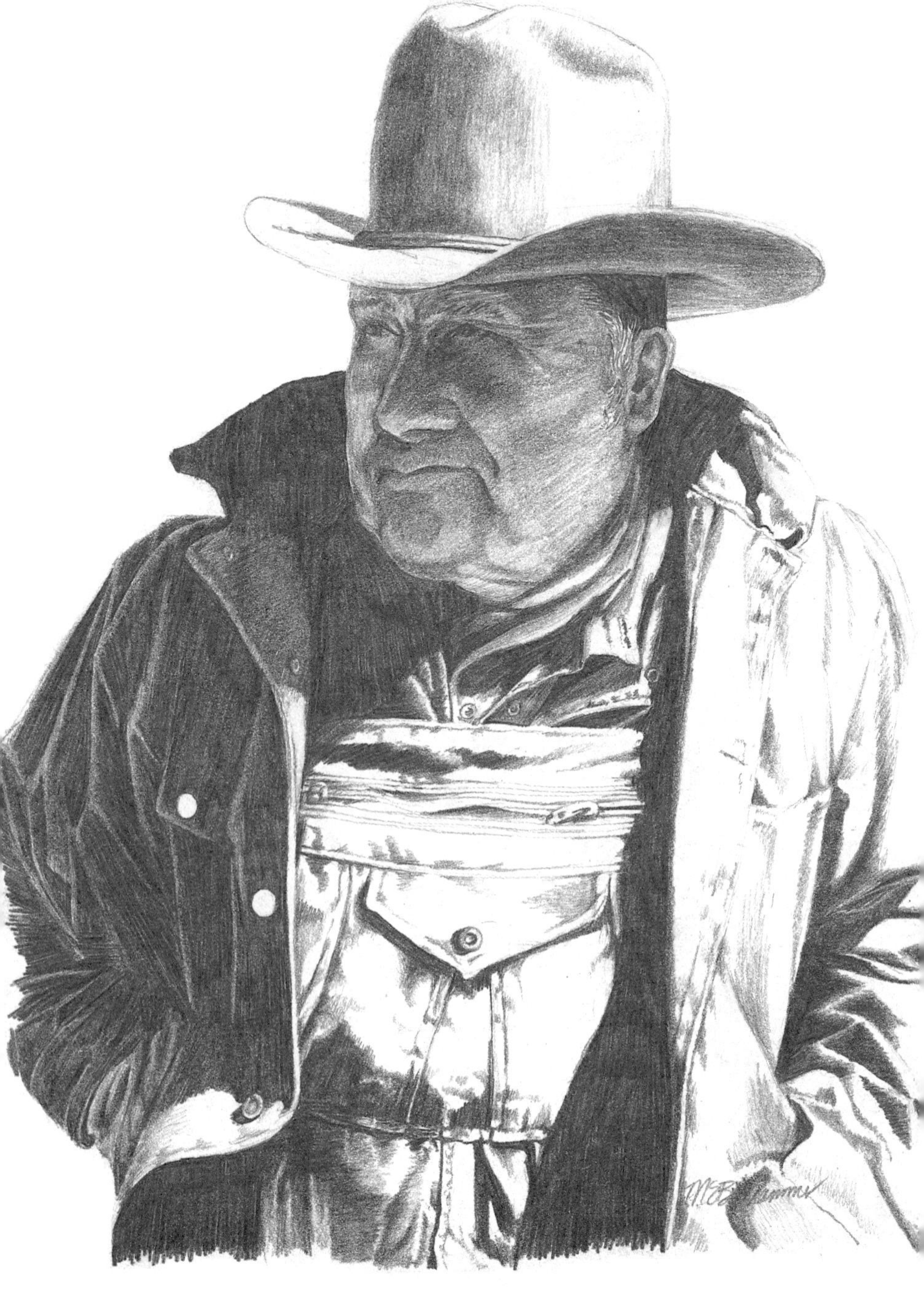

Mist on the Greenleaf

The day was gray as I sat on the hill
overlooking the old Greenleaf Ranch.
The hills and sways were misty and hazy . . .
below lay a small feed patch.

The deer grazes below in the valley of the Ninnescah.
In the distance turkeys gobble,
In my mind as I stop and tarry . . .
I could see through the years gone by.

The haze moved around, bringing a chill,
a light mist began to fall.
Then I realize, I'm not feeling the cold at all . . .
like peering into a crystal ball.

A voice I heard beside me, apparition or real?
An old cowboy on a steeldust grey . . .
I was startled at first, and without voicing my questions
he answered them before they were posed.

"Look into the mist and see how it was
when this country was in its prime.
The redman and buffalo passing . . .
then the longhorn was king of its time.

Over west there passed the Ellsworth Branch
of the old Chisholm Trail.
Further on was the first Catteman's Rodeo
at Kingman in 1899.

The big house on the hill
and the barn with twin silos
standing like sentinels
standing faithfully at their posts.

Surviving all but neglect . . .
soon to be torn down . . .
the ranch is divided among tenants."
With those words he turned and rode away.

Was it a dream or real? I felt like a front row witness . . .
Maybe there dwells on the great ranches
the specters of cowboys past . . .
to guide who would stop and take time and imagine.

Or maybe as we pass, we invest some of our spirit.
If we ride for the brand . . .
something of ourselves will be left with it . . .
to mark the time of our passing.

Or maybe the cowboy fate to watch youth slip away,
Soon all that's left is the grass and spirit,
Invested in a way of life
that is lost as generations pass away.

More Cowboy Definitions

Rude Awakening: Realizing the true number of the 10 you left the dance with . . .

Cowdog: Any breed of dog that a cowboy owns . . . answers to mostly four-letter names.

Insanity: A state of mind that a woman gets in thinking that she can change a man . . .

Liar: A man who claims to understand his woman . . .

Stupid: A man who claims that his woman understands him . . .

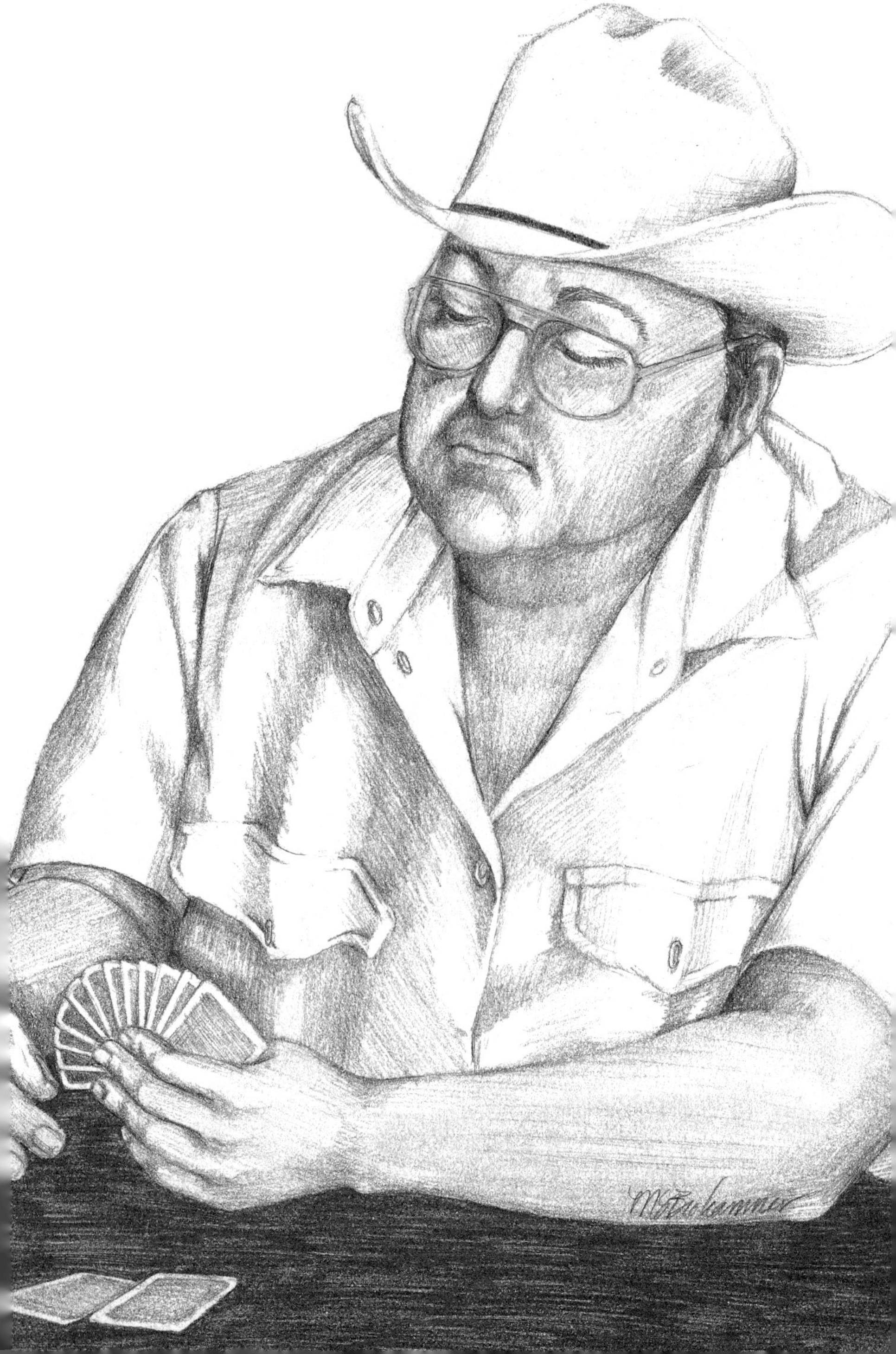

Spring Calving

The temperature's dropping, I feel it in my bones.
The cold seems to chill clear thru my soul.
It started snowing light this morning
and continued past sundown
and now is swirling all around.

I stomp on my boots and stoke up the stove,
want it decent and cozy when I make it back in. . . .
This two-hour routine
is starting to wear mighty thin.

Maybe I'm getting spooky,
nothin's probably brewing.
But I brought up the heifers into the little pasture
and stretched a rope to the barn.

I'll probably be embarrassed
'cause the signs pointed to spring,
The same thing happened last year
when Old John was lost in a late blizzard's wake.

It is a noise that's not really there,
but it is ringing in my ears, I've felt this before.
Better scatter fresh straw in the barn.
If not, in two hours a new calf could be dead.

A battle is starting to brew, the wind whipped on up.
Damn, that's a flash of lightning and thunder,
a bad sign in a blizzard, it can dump snow beyond compare.
Better dry this little feller off and get on back inside.

Many a man's been caught on these plains
when out of the clear blue
a blizzard catches them unaware
and they die cold and blue.

In my younger days I laughed and shrugged off
the fury of the storm,
but that cost me a couple of toes.
I've slowed some now and use experience and not youth.

Brew up another pot of buckle and burn a steak.
Then I'll write another letter and add to the pile
with the others I never sent.
Another two hours and out I go again.

Guess this is a job that many will not do,
especially when you get past the romance to the truth.
I'm not impressin' any ladies and don't feel romantic for hell.
Just out here working getting old and cold.

But spring will come again soon enough
and them calves I birthed with their mamas will move to grass.
I will stretch out on a rock and soak up some sun
till my old bones get thawed out again.

And one Saturday night I will go to the dance
and give Old Emma a twirl.
In my new silk scarf the girls will blush
as my spurs jingle I and whirl them to a tune.

And I will be for one night the hero of them all
and the bane of the drugstore crowd.
There won't be no doubt before this night is out
that I am a cowboy and damn proud.

The Legend

Look there on the horizon
a speck speeding across the plains
Riding with the devil behind
Speeding to carry the parcels with haste

Wind whipping the shirt
determined look to the brow
horse panting and lathered
the joy of speed in his scowl.

Every day doing the impossible
with a devil may care ease
pushing the line to the ultimate
come rain, snow, or gloom of night.

They left out the line
of Indians, bandits,
of stations burnt
and comrades slain.

The adventures these riders lived—
the dash and boldness,
bravado and daring-do—
tugged many a maid's heart string.

Eighteen months of glory
that caught the world's imagination,
Stories that still race the blood,
this was the Pony Express—

The Legend.

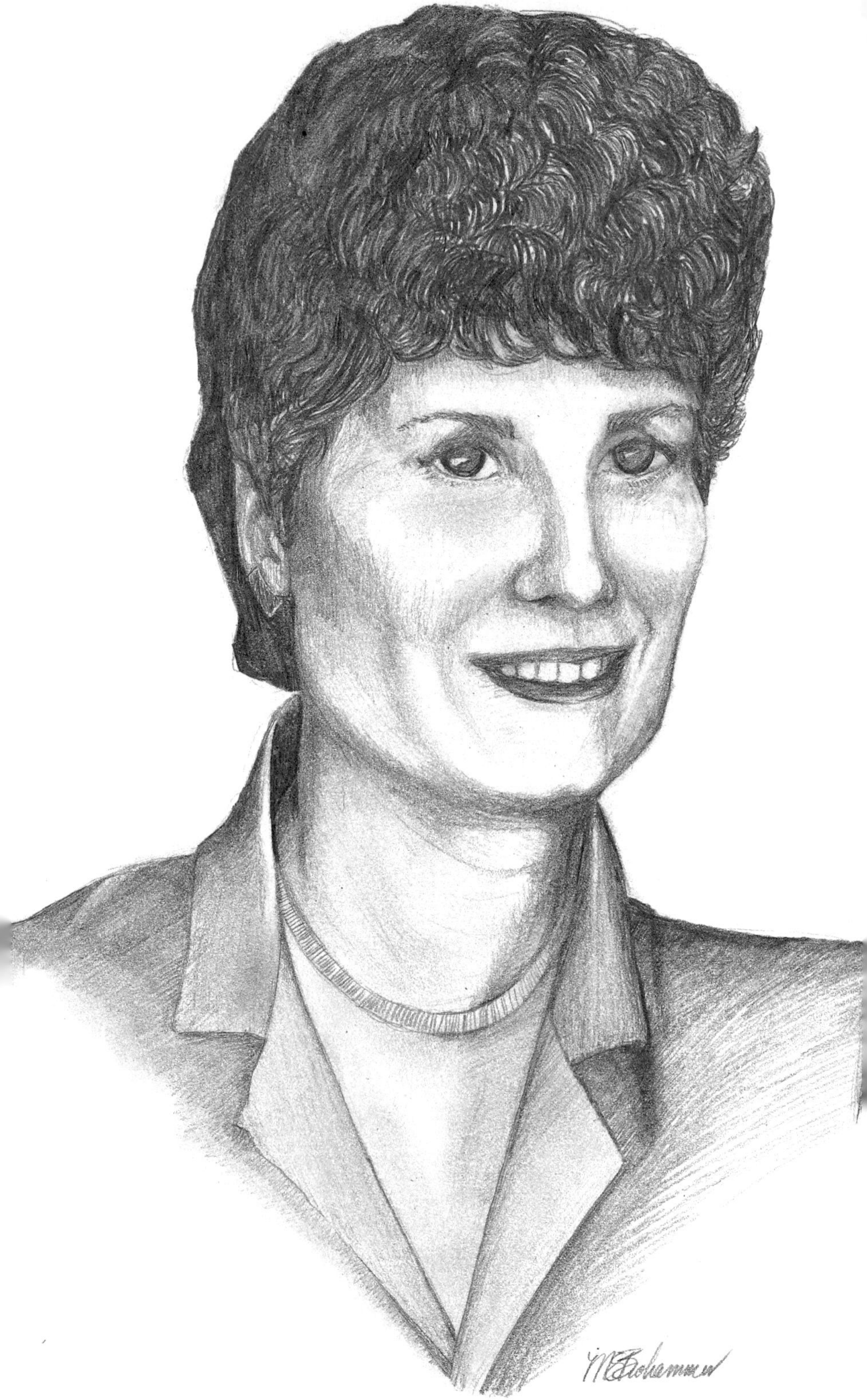

Prairie Love Song

Come take a walk with me through a sea of bluestem grass
waving gently in a Kansas breeze.
Let me tell you my dreams as I hold you close to me
as the cottonwoods dance so free.

We will talk of the future
and plan for you and me
till a shining moon lights the night
as we wish for things to be.

We will silently lie together
on a silky bed of grass
and watch the sun rise together
as the dawning comes to pass.

Come ride with me forever
as we travel never to part,
if we come upon a fallen star
I'll carry it in my pocket over my heart.

Say you will stay with me forever
under a wide blue Kansas sky
and gladly, away I will never roam
from this our Kansas prairie home.

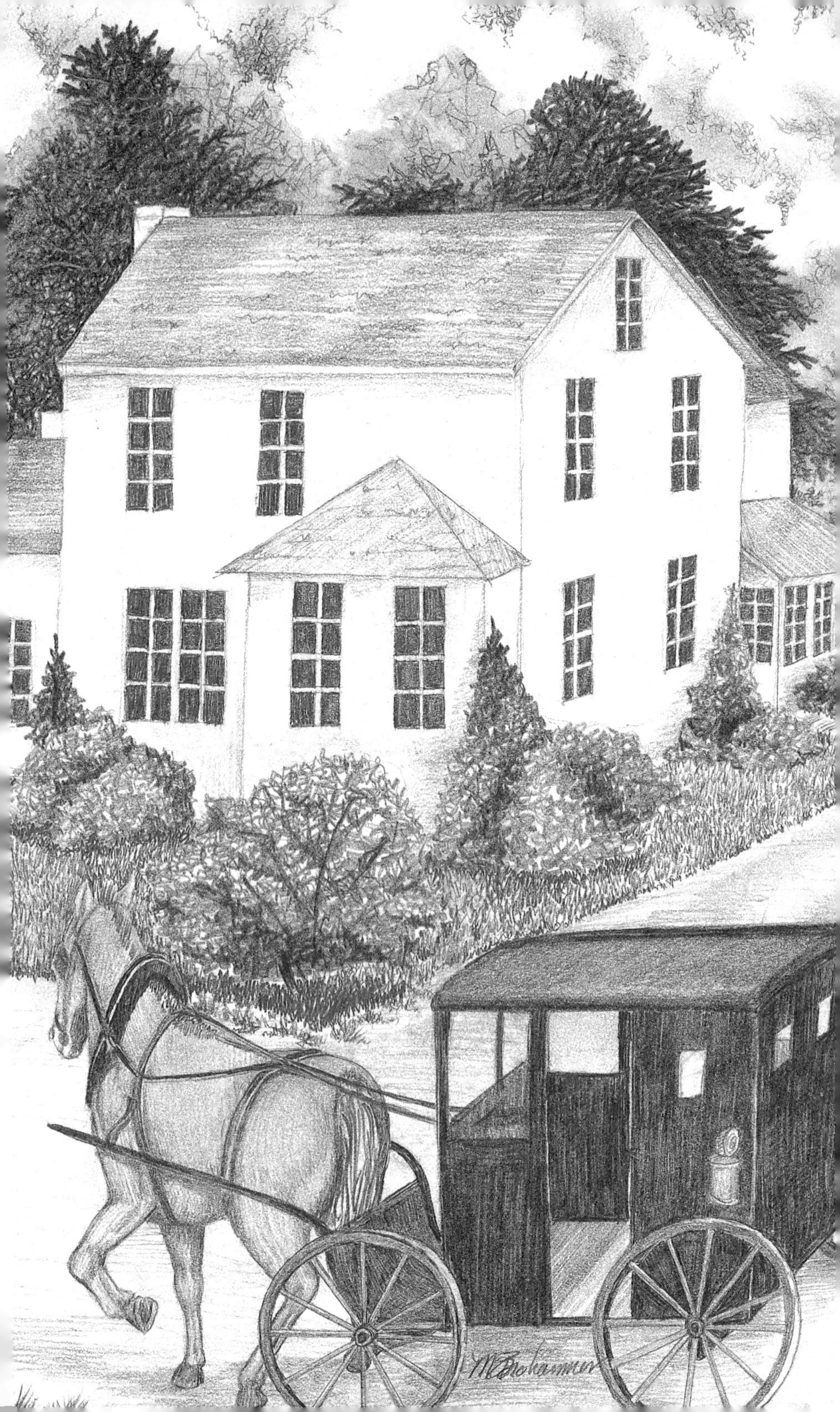

Passin' Along

She stepped quietly into the room, latching the door carefully. Not wanting to raise him from the painless peace he now knew. That elusive sleep that put to bay the creeping cancer that consumed the life from his tired frame. Leaving her the shell that remained.

She smiled as she pushed away a wisp of thin hair that fell across his now furrowed brow. Going back over the years she could see clearly the shy young man she once knew. In her mind's eye she again recalled a youth who pretended not to notice her. Who overcame himself to sweep her off her feet. He never knew his lost shyness she had helped defeat.

He was a tiller of the earth and a child of the Lord and a pretty fair business man. Together united more than twenty-odd years she bore him seven healthy children. Five daughters and two little men.

I don't know, he told her, if I said "I love you" often enough. How much I loved you through all the good times and bad. I want you to know before I go, that I never took you for granted.

He smiled through the pain into eyes full of tears, then said, I'm so proud of the kids and how they have taken my place. But there is one last thing I wish before I leave is to see my first grandchild's face.

He passed on that night, missing his last wish, to walk with God and eternal delights. Piercing the hearts of us left behind. But the lord is merciful and justice comes shining through. For a month he played with her in paradise then escorted her into this world.

A simpler more noble man I have never known. The gap he leaves in all our lives we will feel our whole lives through. Sometimes as we pass on our own paths to the Great Beyond we are privileged to meet someone special who can touch us in a special way.

As the wagons rolled out to the place where we left him in peace and the friends and family all had tears on their cheeks. The only last thing I knew to say as I know he was looking down. I cast my eyes to the cloudy skies and said, "Glen, it was a privilege to know you."

Redjaw Coyote Hunt

My, my, my, says I, as I looked down the lines of his truck. I can't see a dent, a scratch, or a scrape, the work they done was truly first rate.

Who would believe says I to Vic, who stood there grinnin' from ear to ear, that it is possible to make one look like that, a silk purse out of a sow's ear.

Ole Vic swells up with pride, "Ain't it a hell of a deal." Thar won't anyone believe, and I quote, "I rolled her a month ago chasin' that danged old Red Jaw Coyote."

I says well this means you're going to slow down and cut back on your coyote chasin'? He looked at me sort of confused 'n said, "Till this weekend and the chasin' commences."

We loaded up the dog box, put in a gun rack, 'n rigged him out with new radio gear. Then tested it by shoutin' "Load the dogs, boys." And the coyotes of the world shook with fear.

He put her in gear, pulled out of the yard, and we headed 'er north into the Redjaw. About that time Ole Shorty hollers "I got two of 'em spotted in a draw."

We gave 'er hell and assembled around this double section pasture. All the rigs out scoutin' they made 'er on in and said no coyote would slip out of here.

Vic dropped his hounds and so did Joe, and off they went squallin' and bawlin', hot on the fresh scent.

I yelled at Vic as he rolled on in better hold back and givem some room. About that time up jumps a coyote and the chase was on so soon.

Vic yelled in the mike, "What a beautiful sight, it's that light colored cuss that caused all the fuss the last time when I rolled my truck."

He was so excited he stuck on the mike, and as he mashed down on the gas I could hear his gunner yellin' in the background that he should get on this dog's ass.

Down through the draw and up on the hill on and on they were wheelin'. On this ill-fated trip, one pack of dogs, two pickups, and one mangy coyote.

Vic yells on the mike to close the gaps, we're comin' north, no south, we're pushin' him boys, bringin' him west, don't let him get out!

About that time that wily old wolf turns back up a draw, he hunkers down low and tries to sneak out. For about half a minute Vic lost that critter and when he got him back in sight, he mashes down on the throttle and swings up on two wheels and gives his gunner a fright.

You could hear him scream above Vic's rebel yell, "I've got that sucker in my sights, steady now Vic, now bring me on up. I'll show this baby a few tricks."

What happened next was sort of a mess, it happened out of the clear blue. As Vic bore down, the coyote went around a knob of red keel. He locks up his wheels and his gunner gives a squeal.

When he hit that mound, that pickup went down and rolled just like before. Vic swallered his chew and the gunner came in view with his barrel bent neatly around.

We gathered around to pick up the pieces and offer that crew a beer. Theirs all exploded when they pulled the tab and Vic was a little bit shook. He said sober eyed I wonder how the insurance man will put this down in his book.

In critiquin' that run, I says it sure looked like fun, anyways as long as it lasted. But son of a buck, what a string of bad luck. Wasn't it that same coyote and that same mound that rolled you last month?

He replied a little shaken, I thought I had taken that spot on just enough that this time I thought I could make it. But now I thinks I have it figured out. We pulled him on home and parked that mess back down by the body shop. I says on the sly, don't think it will fly. Well at least for a day or two.

But Vic says with a sigh, all's well bye and bye, I think I'll go buy me a Jeep. I jerked with a start, you're shurly not serious, my friend. He grins real big and says, third times charm and that old coyote can't possibly win again.

More Kansas One-Liners

It gets dry in Kansas . . . how dry can it get?

Fellah robbed the bank down at Norwich last week . . . left the money, just took the water bottle.

The cafe sifts out a cup of coffee.

If you complain that your coffee is thick as mud . . . they charge you double for it.

The city fathers over at Garden Plain are looking at the sewer system as a profit center.

A Birthday Visit

A fierce cold wind blew from the plain . . .
Those with a sense were in by the fire's glow.
A lone pickup was parked down by the churchyard,
A solitary figure could be seen standing by a stone.

A weatherbeaten face beneath a stetson pulled low . . .
The piercing cold that laid the country low
Seemed not to even catch the man's attention
as he was lost in conversation.

"Things have not changed much since you were around.
People coming and going, worrying about things,
All wrapped up in what they think's important . . .
Not realizing how soon they must let them go.

Cattle's down and wheat is low,
your brother's still working hard.
And too many people wonder how long
They can hold on before they're sold out
and forced to move to town.

Weather's been tolerable good . . .
Calfs still prance around full of life.
We had crops like you never seen . . .
Sunrise and sets so vivid like the sky's on fire.

The kids you worried about leaving
Are doing right fine, though they miss you.
They're growing and going to school . . .
They will fulfill your dreams in time.

I gotta go now, he said with eyes blurring,
And drop off some packages this evening.
I wish I had been as good a pard to you
As you were for me.

As I go on my way, old pard,
A favor would you do for me?
Keep an eye on my back like you used to,
And when you join the Master on this Christmas Eve . . .

Tell him Happy Birthday for me."

Rounding Up the Strays

I knew an old cowboy, and I do mean old,
When I was growing up he was old.
His weatherbeaten face all brown and wrinkled
Would light up when tickled
Or scare the hell out of you when PO'd.

He rode for outfits from the Brazos to the Toungue
To say he was seasoned wern't making fun.
He could ride anything with hair
And walk away like he never cared,
And laugh . . . when a greenhorn got dumped.

One day we were struck dumb
When this old man's path
Led up the steps of a church house.
He doffed his hat and stepped in . . .
We were shocked and bewildered and followed him.

I think the padre was shocked . . .
To look back at this hard luck lot
Setting in the back with hats in hand
Sheepish looks all around
And a big grin on the old man.

The fires of Hell never burned hotter . . .
Nor Heaven shine so bright,
As the inspired sermon delivered that day.
I think the padre sensed that his chance
At this bunch was only today.

A confused and converted group
Surrounded the old man afterwards.
They got up the nerve to ask
And took the old man to task
As to what got into him that day.

He replied, real tickled,
As to when he came to believe.
His mama taught him early
And took him every Sunday,
And read to him from the family Bible every day.

The secret of his skills
he tried to pass to us every day.
It was the confidence of a man
Who walked along the righteous way
And trusted what the Good Book had to say.

Now I would not fool you, boys,
In believing me to always be upright.
I done my share of straying,
I've seen the critter and walked away
And dance on the edge of Hell's rimrock.

There is nothing you cannot face
Nor a losing side in a race
A bronc so rough . . . Or bull so rank
That can make you run and hide.

Be thankful as you go through life
That elsewhere you weren't forced to abide,
In a boring job and boring life.
Set an example for those around you
And guide who come up behind you.

Now rounding up strays is easy
If you have them all figured out.
No direct move gets them in . . .
It's just gentle move in the right direction
And when in, don't forget to slam shut the gate . . .

To keep them from getting out.

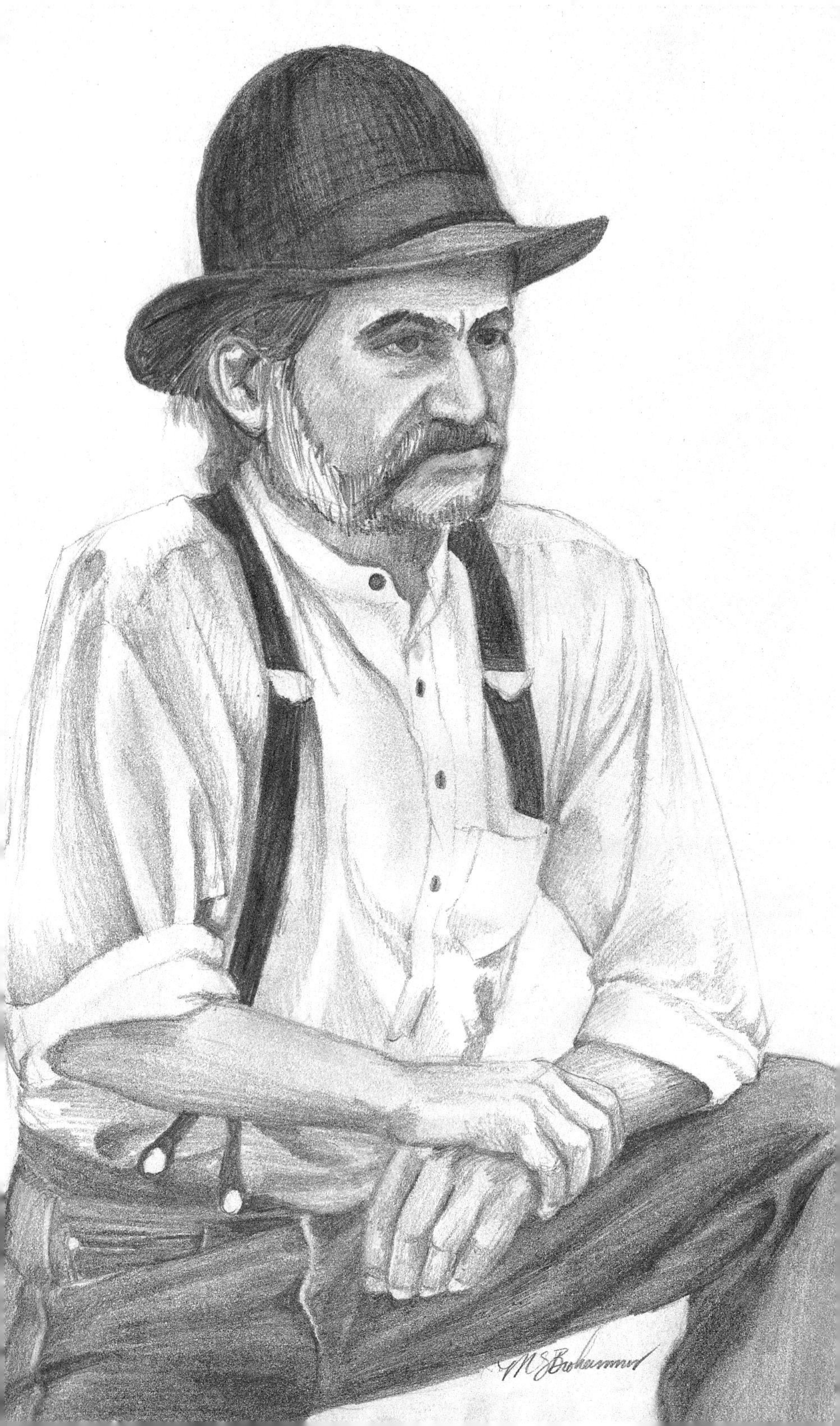

Big Red

He called it "Big Red" . . .
I was somewhat amused,
Then I was a bit perplexed
N' then, to tell the truth . . . I was plain confused.

Now, ole Dave went to town
A-straddle his big old bay,
What he went and traded for . . .
Well . . . I'm ashamed to say.

Now it looked like a big tricycle,
You know, like the little kids ride,
But this had big wheels and was red
And the name "Honda" was on its side.

It was noisy and belched smoke,
Scared the stock half to death . . .
I told him if he used it
It'd be the death of him yet.

Well, he claimed it to be modern
And the horse of the new age
And bragged on its features
Said, among the ranchers it was the new rage.

Now I know Dave was loco'd
And his contraption a mighty big bust.
Told him he couldn't replace a horse
With something that in a junk pile will rust.

Bound and determined he was
To prove the worth of his stead,
So out he went, chasing some cows,
My horse, the dog, and Big Red in the lead.

Now I knew right away
That a wreck was imminently due
When Dave builds a loop
And around the horns he threw.

Dave went to daly
And right away he noticed
That upon ole Big Red
There was nothing to daly to.

I thought it was quite a trick
How he pushed that cow with a rope
Till she decided to turn on him
And run over him on a lope.

Now Dave is back to animals,
Big Red sits in the junk . . .
Told him to go buy a steed that fits the part
But darn'ed if I know what made him come home
With a donkey and a cart!!

Still More Kansas One-Liners

It gets dry in Kansas . . . how dry can it get?

Saw a robin beat the hell out of a redtail hawk trying to hog Mama's birdbath . . .

Water snakes were put on the endangered species list . . .

Instead of canning this year, we waited for a Norther and freeze-dried the vegetables . . .

Silent Night

It was a silent night . . .
Clear and cold like long ago.
The moon and stars shining bright
As old Charlie worked on his goal.

Slippin' the old high back to the ground
Tyin' a ribbon to the horn . . .
With a tag to Jimmy Brown.
Settin' it gently by the door.

As he walked limpin' down the road,
Leadin' that old bay,
Wishin' it weren't so darn cold
As he tied him to the gate . . . at Tommy Ray's.

As he trudged back to his line shack
He took inventory of his Christmas rounds.
Left his spurs for young Zack,
His Mexican riata . . . at Jennie Towns.

A rag doll from an old shirt stuffed with grass
He left for June at the Crossroads Ranch.
She's such a fiery young lass . . .
She'll break more than one cowboy's heart with a glance.

Charlie gave away all of his belongins'
And other things that he made
Till every child in the valley
Had a present for Christmas Day.

He made many winters riding line camps and such
Living life as a drifting saddle tramp
Since a family just wasn't in the cards
Now . . . he is making his final lonely camp.

Bankin' up the stove . . . to warm his old frame,
The chill finally driven from his bones,
He dozed in an old work rocker,
Snoring in peaceful low tones.

He opened his eyes to a young rider
Standing inside the door.
Charlie . . . "It's time to go," he said.
Charlie nodded and said, "I'm ready for dern sure."

A group of people gathered outside that old shack
Grateful for the simple gifts he brought.
They found him cold . . . by his empty pack,
Gone home . . . to the final camp he sought.

For years they talked of that terrible drought
When all the grass withered like blight.
How hard times had stolen their holiday cheer,
And how one cowboy . . . named Charlie . . .
Saved Christmas . . . on that cold *Silent Night*.

More Cowboy Truisms

Ridin' a buckin' bronc spooked by a hillside full of rattlesnakes will make you a world class rider real fast.

Sinnin' can't be done proper without lots of practice. Watch out for them that are too good at it.

Walking in another man's boots may not be so enlightening as it might get you shot.

It is seldom remembered how the burr got under the saddle . . . but the hell that it caused will be remembered forever.

Snaky

Riding for a brand new brand
Out yonder in the gypsum hills . . .
Checking fence with the new boss,
Not looking for any thrills.

Riding a broncy bronc
That was only just green broke.
My mind was on the work . . .
Between me and the boss not much was spoke.

This new country looked snaky,
And if you like 'em like me . . .
Then you will understand that I'm a big shaky
About buzzin' things next to me.

Now we had just topped a bluff
And started over the crest
When something went to buzzing
And made my heart pound in my chest.

The bronc blew up,
And down the hill we went crowhopping
And I am hanging on for dear life,
Bouncing, swaying, and beboppin'.

I made it to the bottom in one piece
And looked back to check on the boss.
He was sitting there laughing,
Still on his unmoving horse.

I was relieved that he wasn't hurt,
So I tried to warn him
Off that rattler . . .
Unseen in the brush!!

He laughed in a gleeful tone,
Said not to worry about it at last.
That buzz was from his cellular phone
And he just got a call from his staff.

Now I am all for progress,
I'm not stuck in a rut.
Things that makes the job easier . . .
Hell, I'm not no funny dud.

But I still can't get that bronc
From acting like the strawberry roan . . .
Cause he still won't accept
A cowboy with a cellular phone!!

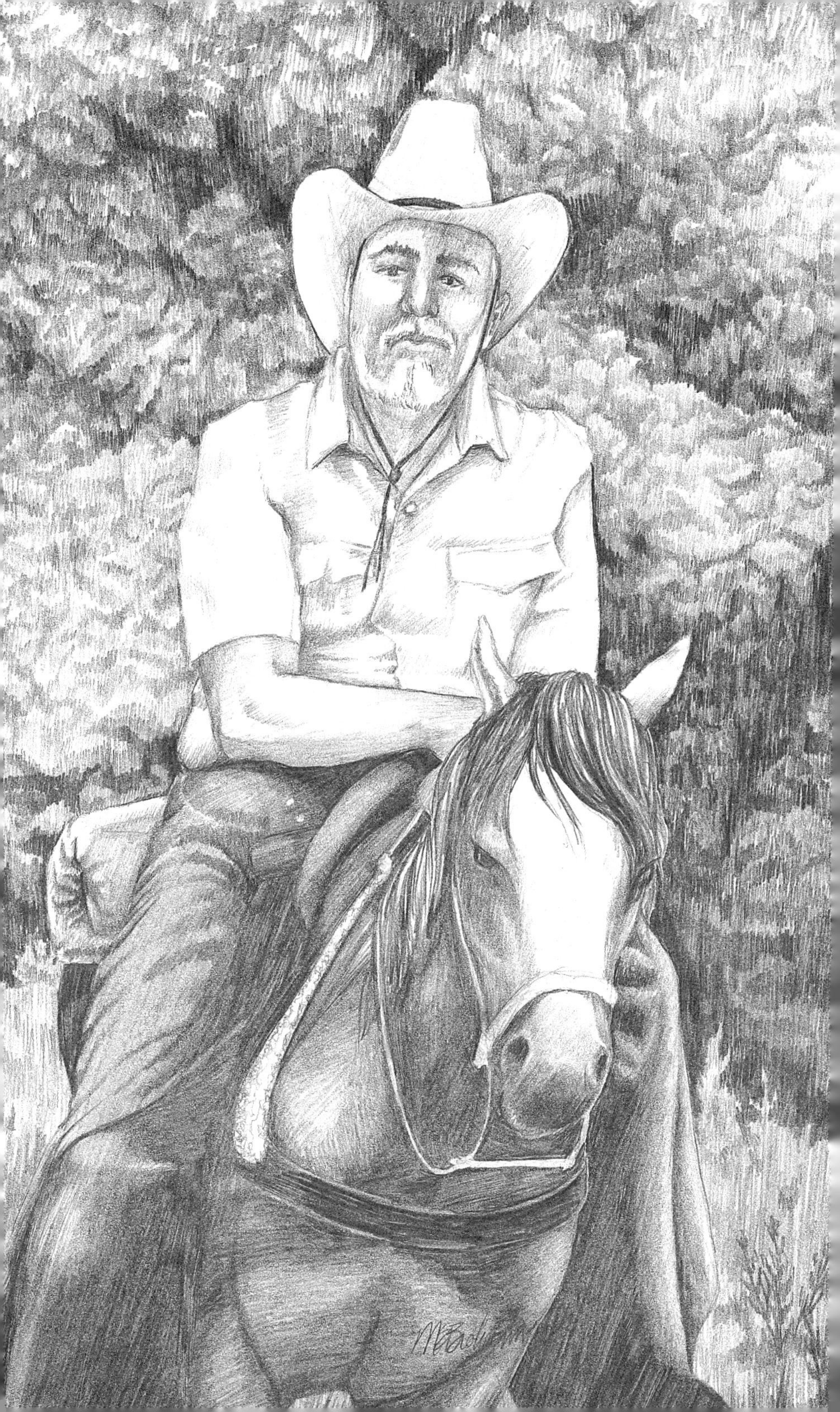

Nightmare

I don't recollect the first time I dreamed it . . .
Seems it has been with me since I was a pup.
I never knew what to make of it,
I've lived with it all this time . . .
I never connected it to anything in my past.
It always seemed to be the strongest
When some disaster was about to strike.
It took a while to decipher it out
Whether it was a dream . . . nightmare . . .
Or, preview to a grim fate.

He was big and black and had all the worst traits
Of any bad bull I have ever seen,
The ugliest . . . meanest . . . son of a bull . . .
That ever bucked in a rodeo show.
But, I could see that there was more . . .
Most bulls will perform then go about his business
Living a life of ease.
But, this belligerent brute was different . . .
He had other needs!

Every time I'd see him among my dreams
I woke with a cold sweat . . . trembling . . .
Not knowing what he meant to me.
He is black as sin and bigger than most . . .
Why, he would tip the scales over two thousand.
In his souless eyes there is evil . . .
Looking into them will chill to the bone,
Just like meeting the Devil in his own home.

Truly he is the spawn of Satan
And exists to destroy good cowboys.
Not satisfied with just throwing you
And making you eat the dirt,
He is there to stomp you and hook you,
And destroy you if he can . . .
Claiming you for his own.

I rode the circuit for years and years,
Never saw him in the flesh . . . *My Ghost Bull.*
A forewarning messenger of fear and disaster . . .
I had to ignore him when he appeared.
Throughout my riding years, dismissed it as superstition,
The haunt of a rodeo man's worst fears.

I was riding high at Kingman,
Drew a bull that I have never seen,
Only heard about by reputation.
Undefeated . . . raised in the nation . . .
Wild and tough and mean as they come.
His fame was not as much reputation as description,
A score card of the deeds he has done
To those with the nerve to brace him.
One man broken for life, others injured and bleeding,
Two men he killed outright,
And, every time a new victim went down
And the crowd hushed without a sound
He would stroll around the arena . . . looking . . .
As if searching someone in particular out . . .
Searching Me Out.

My darkest dream searching me out . . .
My destiny rushing toward me,
My nemesis seeking me out.
The specter I tried to ignore.

I went to the pen to check my draw out . . .
And stopped stock still in my tracks.
There he was . . . staring at me standing all alone.
It hit me like a bullet and I froze where I stood.
My nightmare in the flesh . . . I did not know what to say.

The contractor's words came through a fog.
He said, "Son, this is your ultimate test.
To survive this ride you are surely the best.
He comes out honest," he said, "then explodes.
He is fond of turning right . . . But, take care
On the nights when he is hell on earth
He will go left . . . But the thing that is the worst
Is when you're down . . . and most bulls quit
This brute goes into a fit."

He went on, serious as a judge,
"When you come off . . . whether eight seconds or less
Do not tarry on the ground.
Remember those who have gone before,
Get to the fence as fast as you can . . . do not hesitate . . .
Be late and it is for certain you face a grim fate."

To say that I was shaken is a world class understatement.
Normally I do not drink . . . But that night
I killed a pint of Jack . . . waking up a little shakey.
Making it through the day . . . minute by minute . . .
By the time the show was about to begin . . .
I made up my mind to face it.

Years of torment and fear I deal with tonight
Then I remember advice that an old rider shared.
When fear is destroying your concentration
And turning you into a wreck, reach way down inside . . .
And pull your nerve up by the neck.

Look that demon in the eye and laugh in his face.
Take the gauntlet up . . . use it to your advantage,
Turn your fear to concentration,
Trust your experience and skill . . .
Even if the tide turns against you.
Give it all you've got . . . use your will.

I settled on him good and tight
As I rosined up the rope.
Someone slapped me on the back and said,
"God ride with you boy." At that
I nodded my hat and out the chute we went,
Hoping he would go right . . . knowing he would go left.

I knew exactly what it meant . . . signaling the worst . . .
This brute who had never been rode
Had marked me for death.
I seemed to know each move he would make
For I rode him for years in my dreams.
I lost all sense of time . . . whether one second or eight . . .
It just seemed to be the longest I have ever made.

The buzzer rang and I went to the ground,
I heard the crowd give a roar.
Then, I started running for the fence . . .
A half second ahead of death's door.
It seemed as every ride of my life
Was packed in this one outing.

Memories were made that night
And many still talk about it.
I sometimes think and wonder
Was it just a bull that I rode
Or, my *fear* that was defeated.

Openers of the West

It tugs on the heart
Builds people's yearnings
Lures the imagination
And fires the soul

Go West! Young man, Go West!
It's where opportunity lay
Where you can make your fortune
That's what they all say

The line of wagons leave St. Joe
bound for Oregon way
There are others who take the cut
and go to Californi-a

They say you can pick up gold
Right out of the river's edge
as big as hen eggs
Makes you a fortune in days

Here I stand by the Missouri
The excitement is in the air
Children hollar and women shout
as the Pony Express rider passes near

Historians will write of this
And put each thing in its place
What made a whole country's pulse race
each time a rider mounted and pulled away

It captures the imagination
as the frontier stubbornly gave way
of a nation growing westward
in its adolescent days

Inspired by the great enterprise
their spirit will be remembered no less
as the intrepid postal riders
of the legendary Pony Express

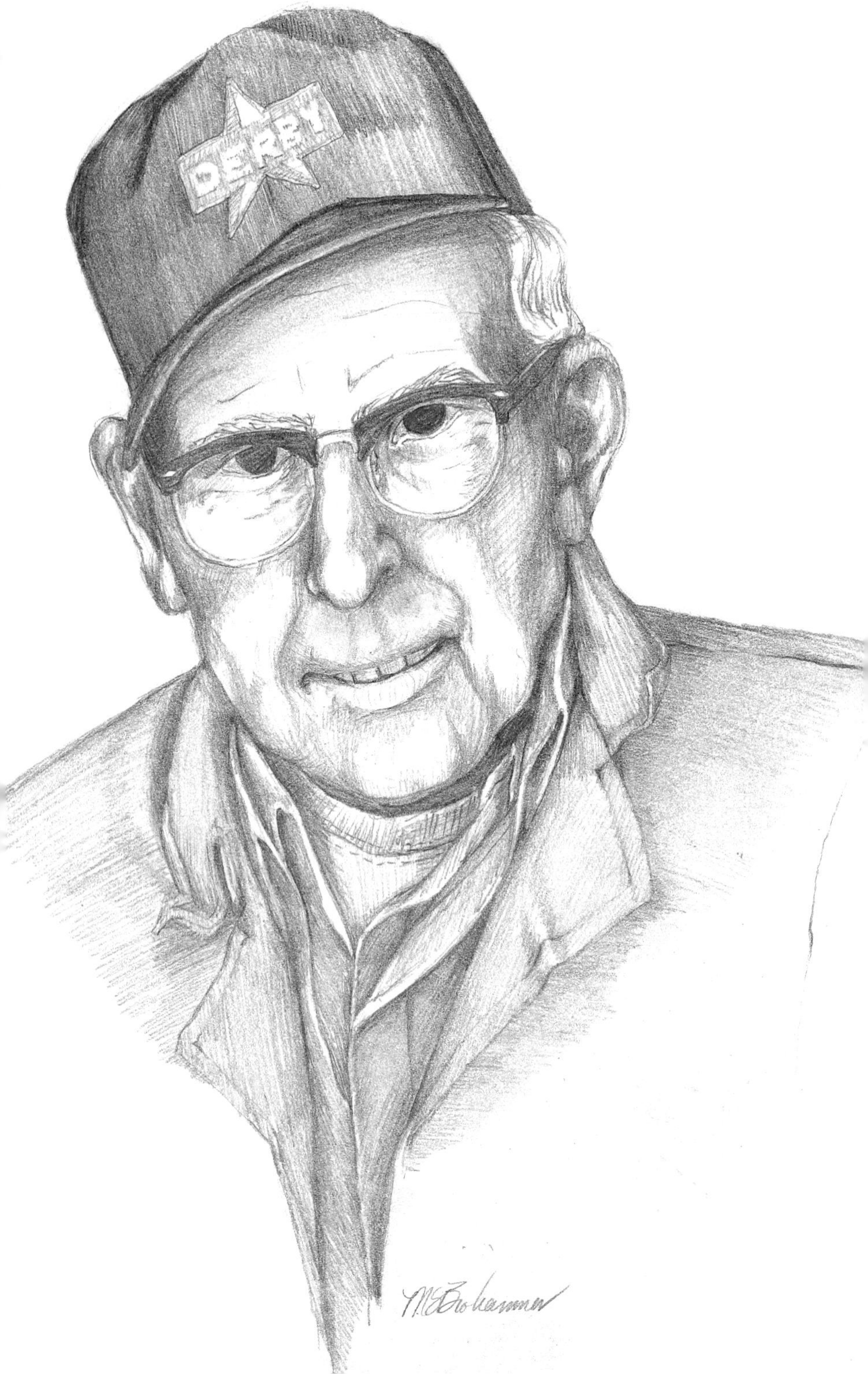
DERBY

An Old Cowboy's Final Comment

He said, Well, Old Dunny, it's been a long trail
This brush popin' just seems to get harder every year.
Did I ever tell you about the first bronco I forked?
Now, you stop me if you have heard this before.

I was green, just off the farm . . .
When I signed on with Slaughter's outfit.
The foreman told me if I would stick to it
He'd make a top hand out of me yet.

That Old Dun they cut out for me to ride
Had a mean look in his eyes.
And when I jumped in the saddle
He left me reaching for the sky.

But I stayed with him
Till I learned not to be throwed . . .
Through plain old cowboy determination.
I could finally put on one heck of a show.

I always planned to get a place of my own,
Get a wife and have kids.
But you know man's plans are well intentioned,
But many times end up on the skids.

Here I am . . . still riding for the brand
When most retire and quit.
But, Dunny, what we do,
If we had to play bingo for entertainment.

I'd be about half crazy.
They would ship you off to the sale
And no one would even believe me
When I told them all my tales.

But you suit me just fine.
Like me, you have slowed your gait,
Not as nimble as in our youth.
We will be quite a sight
When we pull up to Saint Pete's gate.

We found them there together
Where Old Dunny fell.
A peaceful look on the old man's face,
Just like he stopped to rest a spell.

The Boss spoke over his grave.
A top hand to the end,
He might not have been as fast
As in his younger days had been.

A lesson to be gained from his solitary life . . .
He would not quit . . . when most would pack it on in . . .
To die as he lived . . . Made an impression on the men.
We all made a vow right as we stood over him,
To live life full to the end.

Dad's Shop

It sets in the middle of the yard . . .
probably the third thing you'll see.
The first being the old farm house,
Second, the old barn by the tree,
Then, straight across is "Dad's Shop."

A too-small building surrounded by stuff,
the LP tank and fuel trailer is seen.
Old parts from things ancient and new.
An old discarded coke machine
and stubs of old welding rod strewn.

To enter here is not easy
cause there is a path kinda here and there.
A bench piled a full foot high
of tools and odd repairs
and we sorted piece by piece.

Pulling from what seemed endless piles
within what seemed to be chaos . . .
started to take some order . . .
deposited here and there . . .
the story of a life told.

As each item is sorted
into beer flats for the auction to be sold,
out of the past the stories unfold
and memories start flowing fondly along.
Just like a movie the story is told.

A piece from a car that Gene once owned.
Parts for Kevin's CB radio . . .
A hoist that Pat loaned to ease the load . . .
The blue rock thrower he gave Joe . . .
Even some things that Dave left behind.

Echoes of Shorty
giving advice
or a hand here and there
with a lip full of skoal
in his hand a Hanley beer.

A part for every machine
that was ever used on this farm.
A drawer full of files we found,
bought from Boeing surplus by the pound!
And wrenches of every style and kind
produced in the last hundred years.

As the shed is stripped of all items
and each memory and story did unfold,
we all stood in wonder . . .
As how all of this could fit
in such a small humble abode.

One son looks at the walls and realizes
and it strikes him odd in a way,
"I've never seen these walls stripped bare and clean.
We even split the little tractor in here
one long ago day."

Now all cleaned out and ready
for the ladies to serve coffee and pie.
This lonely old building seemed vacant and shy,
ready to take on this new job
for what seemed a minor role.

It sorta brought a tear to our eyes.

For this was the center
of something called a "family farm."
It contained the story of a lifetime . . .
without it all would have ground to a stop.
Now it sets empty, just a cold old shop.

But life goes on and the family left that day.
It could be used to park Grandma's car,
maybe even torn down some day.
We will always refer to that spot in the yard
as "Dad's Shop."

I turn and vision a smile . . .
Blue jeans, Co-op cap, greasy hands,
and leave a lump in the throat
and swallowing hard.

God Don't Like Mobile Homes

Let me expand on a point
That is common knowledge out on the plains.
It is a familiar subject at the cafe
But has failed to be debated or addressed
By religious scholars or doctors of sociologists.

God don't like mobile homes, on this point I will repeat
God don't like mobile homes.
This is not a rash statement,
It's been formed by years of experience.

Let us look historically
And analyze like a scientist.
Let us seek a "reasonable" explanation
Why this fact exists.

As the storm clouds gather
On a hot spring day
You know to avoid the mobile home park
For there is a tornado on the way.

And trailers draw tornados like a magnet.
You see it time and time again
When you watches the reports on TV.
The trailers were plucked like a hen.

If you see regular houses hit
And you look close to the areas around
You can bet that mobile homes were near.
The twister just missed them by bad aiming.

Maybe it's the static of concentrated metal
Or ionization of multiple antennas and dishes
Or vibrations of cars on jacks.
Maybe a mass flush created a low pressure situation.

Or the effect of concentrated charcoal burners
Or atmospheric impact of a gallon of picked eggs
Flows of hot air by gossiping over the fence,
Or the storm of protest by surrounding residents.

Now don't judge me harshly
For the observations that I make.
I have nothing against someone
For the shelter that they take.

Many of my neighbors have them . . .
For some they are temporary housing . . .
The circumstances are circumstantial . . .
And this is a circumstantial case.

However, many agree with me that . . .
God don't like mobile homes.

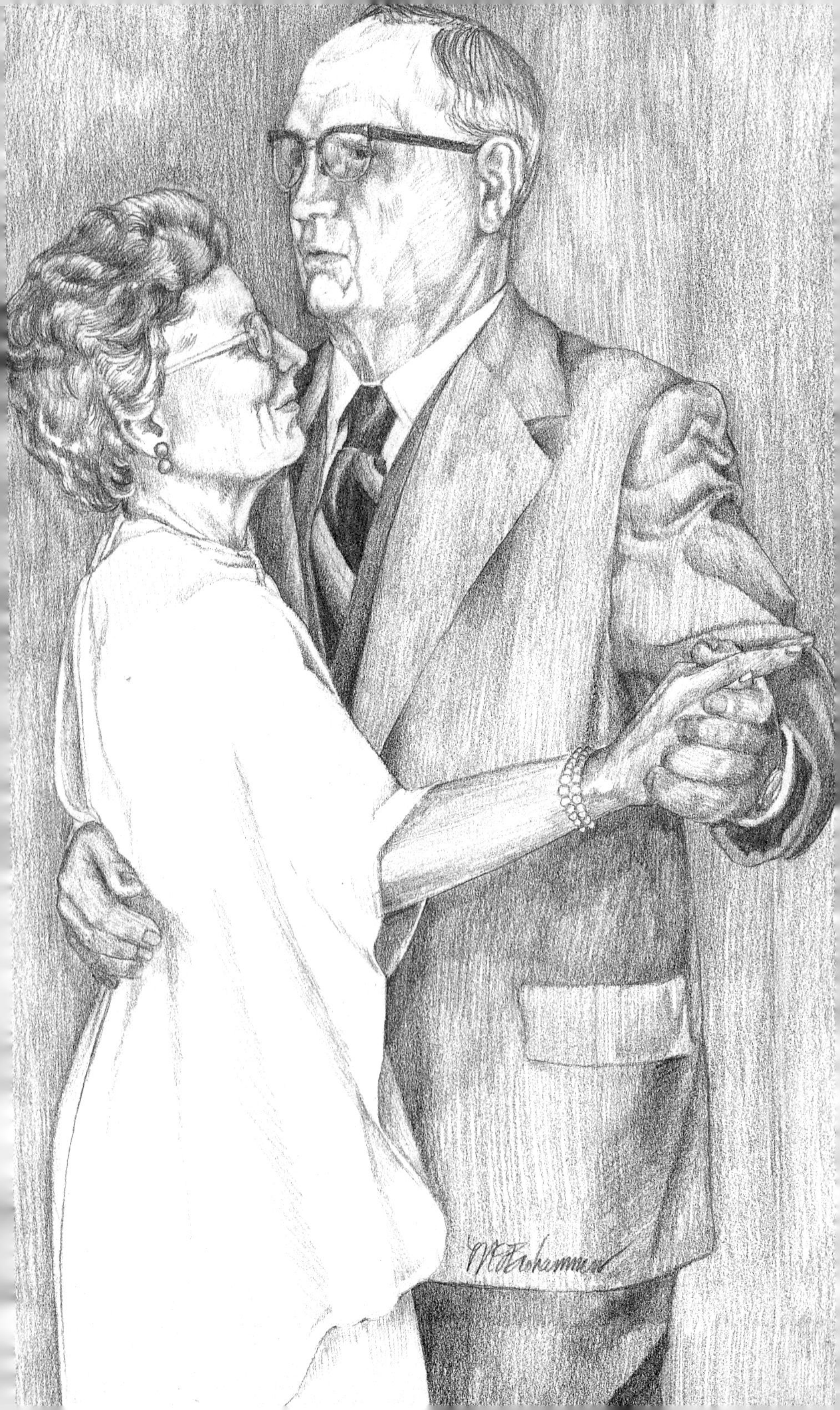

Dance at the Grange

The band was playin' a lively old tune
With young and old at the dance.
'Twas the social event of the season,
They weren't all there just by chance.

Across the room a young stockman looked
And the slip of a girl caught his eye.
He decided right then and there
Not to let opportunity pass him by.

He took her out on the dance floor,
Her moves were quick and light,
He matched her move for move
And magic happened that night.

Fifty years later on another dance floor
Their steps were still quick and light,
Dancing as if made for each other
As they went through life side by side.

I look back to that dance at the Grange,
In Bayneville the hall still stands.
From that one night a family came
When my Grandma met my Grandad.

Still More Cowboy Truisms

You never remember the things that go smoothly. The best memories and laughs come when things go plumb to hell.

The world's biggest lie is "I'm from the government and I'm here to help you."

A lot of people won't think an idea is worth a damn . . . until they are convinced it is their idea.

New boots will always find the freshest cowpie in the lot . . .

The quickest way to start a fight is to mess with a cowboy's hat.

Big Daddy's Last Harvest

It was a typical Kansas summer day
the sun . . . it was blazing hot!
Not a cloud in the sky . . .
Perfect for cutting wheat.

I sat in the field driving the truck
and pondered what this day meant.
To the rest of the world
it is just another day God sent.

The wheat is ripe for the cut . . .
The harvest rush is in full swing.
But, I can tell in my bones . . .
that this is no ordinary day.

Big Daddy—Frank Kyle, has been farming this quarter
since coming back from the war.
Now, he's giving it up
making his work load lighter for sure.

Now, Frank is not moving so well
and figures to slow down a bit.
Time lately has not been treating him kind . . .
And he can't do much without resting a spell.

I just watched him take five minutes
to climb up in the cab . . .
once the combine is moving
he is feeling back home again.

Working again on the land that he loves.
He is wearing a satisfied grin . . .
He will work as many hours as it takes
to bring this harvest in.

Now a tear clouds my eye
as I sit and watch him roll on by.
I see the smile on his face and realize
what this all means to him.

From the day of his birth
he was bound to the earth . . .
His roots anchored deep in this fertile soil
and support his family a must.

He knew full well
what finishing this will be.
This his last harvest will be . . .

And it was.

Still More Cowboy Definitions

Dependable: The dog will always sit in the gate . . . when you don't want him there.

Murphy's Law: Constant companion of those engaged in agriculture . . .

Van Dyke's Theorem: Proves Murphy was an optimist . . .

Expert: A person who know a lot about a little . . .

Authority: A person who knows more and more about less and less . . .

Specialist: A person who knows so much about so little that he knows everything about nothing . . .

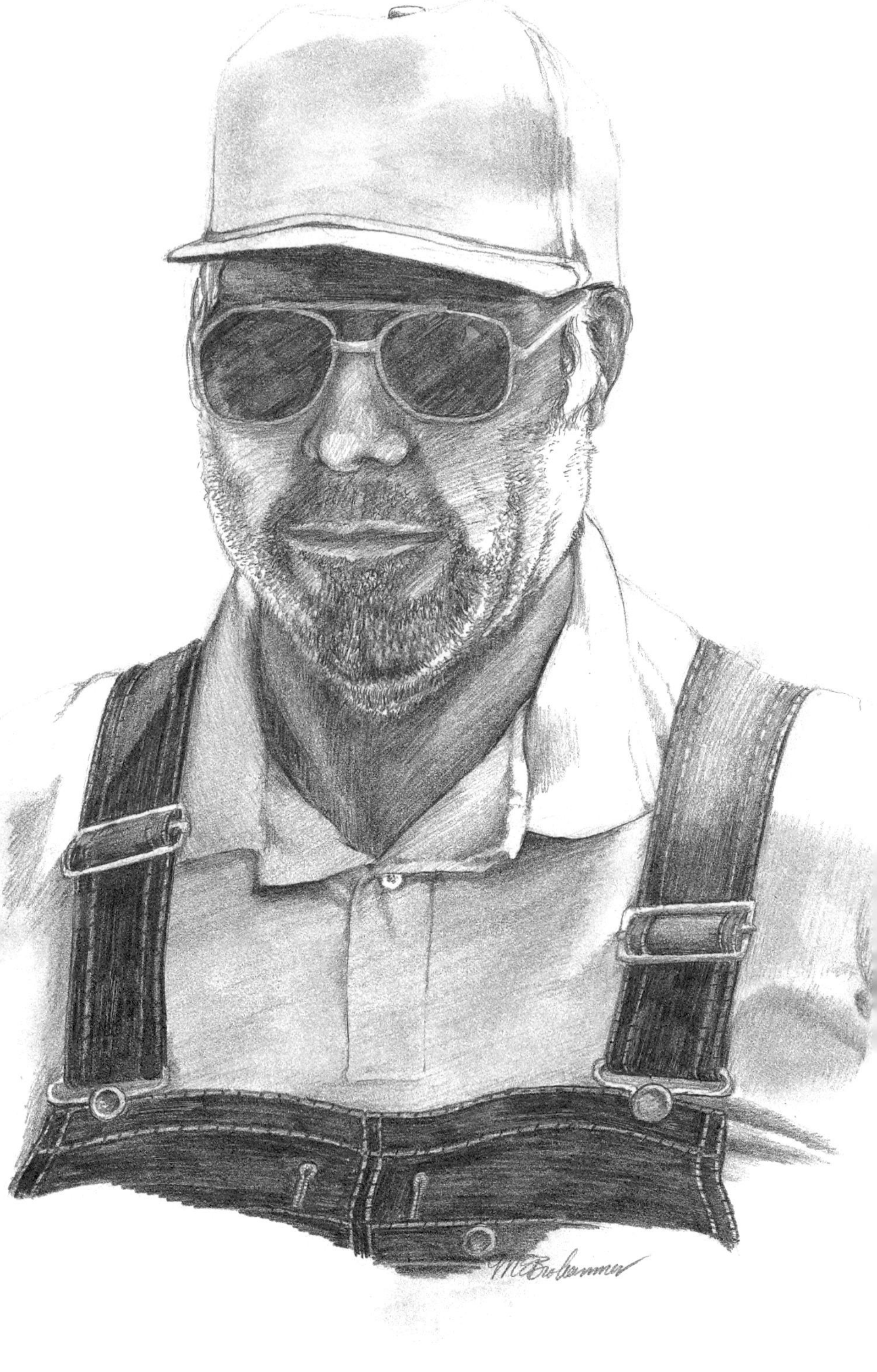

Full Bloom

Cherry trees a bloomin'
in the spring for all to see
At our Nation's Capitol in Washington D.C.

Indian paintbrush and wildflowers abound
In the mountains in Wyoming,
Montana and many states around.

Texas bluebonnets, beautiful roadsides
Or, when the bloom is on the sage
Give variety to the state and has for many an age.

In summertime Kansas sunflowers
are everywhere to be found.
Their happy little faces
simply follow one around.

Arizona cactus in a painted desert
give a picture so serene.
Everyone must experience it
if only in their dreams.

After the blossoms wonderful fruits abound . . .
Georgia peaches, Washington apples,
Michigan cranberries,
Florida oranges, California strawberries . . .
many more can be found.

But, what is so rare as a day in June
When the feedlots of Dodge City . . .
are in full bloom!

Mom's Things

Poems by Charlotte Ringer, My Mom

Memories of Mom

This little lady we call "Mom" . . .
Some call Grandma, Sister, Aunt Mae,
neighbor or friend . . . 'tis true . . .
This silver haired lady with eyes so blue.
This bundle of dynamite aged with such dignity and grace,
That genuine "special" smile always on her face.

Many happy years were spent with Dad.
Remember their Golden Anniversary . . .
Wow! What a party we all had.
Some times were hard, that's true . . .
But, she was a trooper . . . made the best of it . . .
While seeing all of us through.

Mom loved life . . . love youth . . .
Always interested in their dreams.
She delighted in tucking us "under her wings."
Encouragement, faith, hope and love . . .
The rosary, her favorite prayer, to God above.

Let's remember the wonderful years spent on her way . . .
Not the rough painful days while fading away.
Mom loved life and lived it to the fullest . . .
Loved music, dancing, clothes, reading, cards, quilting,
sewing, crossword puzzles, sports, bingo and gingerbread boys.
My! How we'll miss that little Buick with her honking around.
Off to Church, Golden Chain, EHU or a rummy game . . .
My how she did enjoy those superbowl games.
The fun and the fellowship of friends will always remain.

Her Creator reached down from Heaven . . . all too soon . . .
But with love, took her somewhere *"just beyond the moon."*
There to greet her was Dad with outstretched hand . . .
A gleam in his eye "Been waiting to ask you again" . . .
"Could I have this dance for the rest of my life.
Now, I can *waltz across heaven* with you in my arms."

Good-bye Mom, thank you for caring and sharing . . .
We love you . . . we'll miss you . . .

Big Daddy

Frank Kyle . . . What a man
Lover of life . . . Keeper of the land
Generous heart . . . Good neighbor
Friend to young and old as well
Hard workin' . . . Hard cussin'
Loved good food . . . Cold Coors in a can
Loved huntin' . . . Loved fishin'
A true family man
Loved by many . . . Good to all
His handle . . . "Big Daddy"
Fits well . . . Says it all

Quilt of Love

One day long ago, a pattern was found
in a magazine called Hoard's Dairyman . . .
it's probably no longer around.
Sent for it, stamped the blocks, it was ready to go . . .
Who in particular I did not know.

Grandma Ohnemiller was visiting one bright sunny day.
"Need something to work on" she did say.
So out came the blocks . . . she embroidered away . . .
"Now I lay me down to sleep . . .
Heavenly angels guard my sleep" they say.
Each block touched with love . . . each one worked with care,
Each with an animal . . . or a baby so dear.
The blocks were done, rolled up, stored away . . .
Waiting for a special someone . . . someday!!

One day Grandma Becker was scrounging around . . .
The perfect material just had to be found.
Twas pink rosebud material of Aunt Clara's found folded away,
bought to be used . . . well, maybe someday!!

The quilt was set together with care.
Now, all it needed . . . a little quilting here and there.
You can bet each stitch Grandma made with love and care!!
She probably laughed at the animals . . . even the bear!
Wondering whose tiny baby it would cuddle with glee.

You can be sure the grandmas see us today . . .
Now, we all know their working away . . .
was done for the first baby of Noal and Jená.

The quilt and its story of love
was given to Jená from Great Aunt Charlotte
and those Ohnemiller girls in heaven above.

Bucky's Christmas Visit

Once upon a time . . . not so long ago
Our neighbor dog named Bucky
Would come to play and visit . . .
When, we'd never know.

Sometimes he'd come at night . . .
And howl at the full moon.
Or, wake the coyotes and their pups
Twas such a frightful tune.

Sometimes in the daylight he'd come
Just to play and fool around.
His favorite food . . . biscuits and gravy . . .
Or any food that could be found!

Bucky's special Christmas visit
Will in our minds remain.
The Christmas night he came,
Curled up in the Stable . . .
Keeping Baby Jesus, Mary, Joseph
and himself warm
Like the animals did that First Christmas morn.

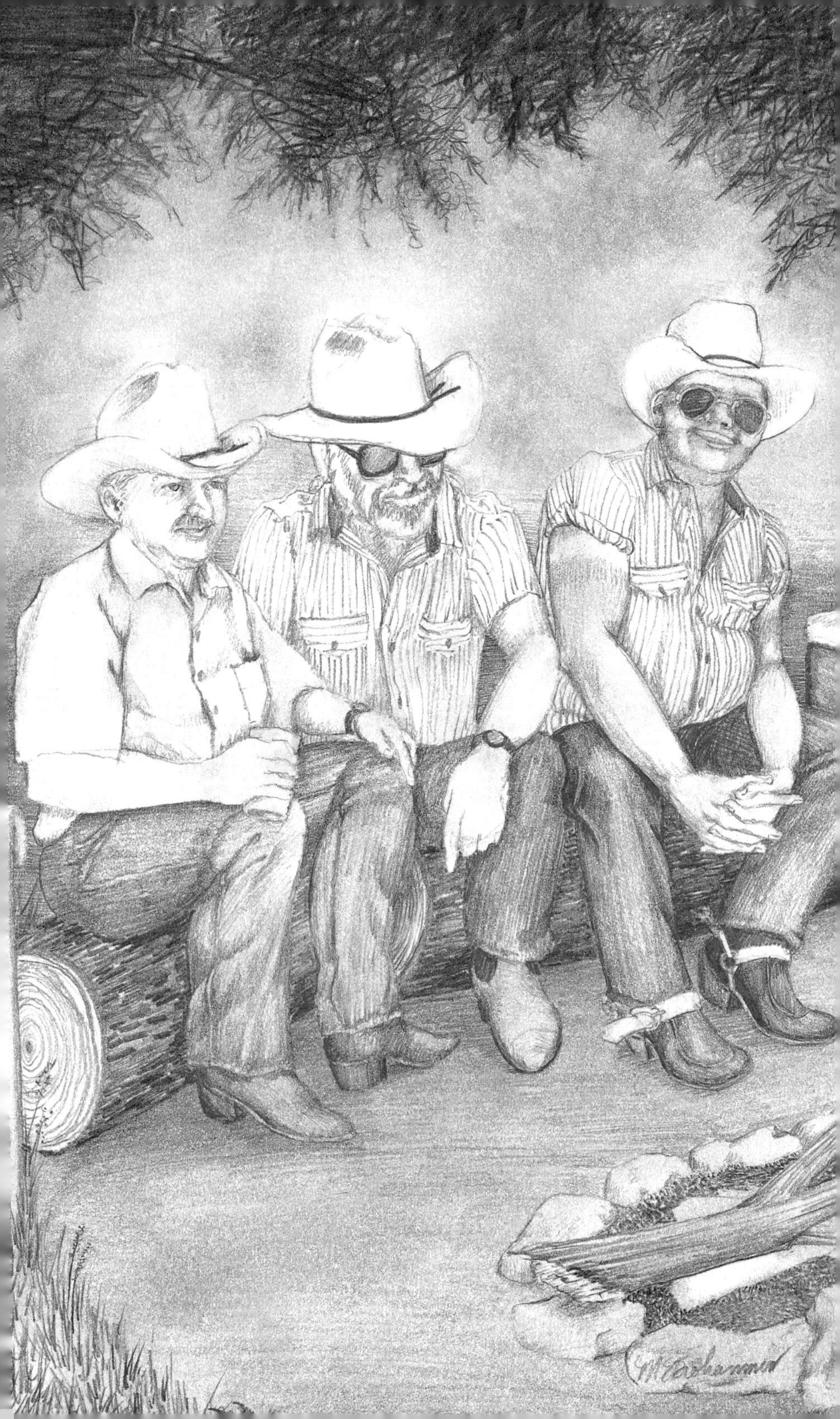

True Friends

True Friends are wonderful indeed.
We laugh, cry, pray . . whatever the need.
Daily we thank the Lord up above.
His help binds us together with love.

Years bring us fun and laughter . .
Simple joy we have . . just being together!
Seasons of our lives are often told.
We hate to admit we may someday be old.

Sometimes a sword pierces our heart . .
When something in our lives goes awry . .
Shaking our heads . .
We may even ask God, WHY?

Faith and friendship are constant . .
regardless of circumstance.
Love ties us together . . nothing is left to chance.
True Friends are there . . whatever the need.
Helping each other in thought, word, and deed.

Having True Friends is a privilege untold.
Some never know the feeling true friendship holds.
TRUE FRIENDS have always enriched our lives.
Without it . . how does one ever survive.

Contact Information

The Author
Roger Ringer
Wildfire Ranch Productions
1660 S 343rd W
Cheney, KS 67025
Ph. 316-540-0105

The Artist
Martha Brohammer
P.O. Box 673
Clearwater, KS 67026
E-mail: Qanartc@sktc.net

A selection of the full-page illustrations have been reproduced as prints. Contact the artist for more information.